FEMALE.
Likes Cheese.
COMES WITH DOG.

W0010255

FEMALE.
Likes Cheese.
COMES WITH DOG.

Stories About Divorce,
Dating, and Saying "I Do"

LAUREN PEACOCK

LL ENTERTAINMENT

Copyright © 2020 Lauren Peacock

All rights reserved.

No part of this book may be reproduced, or
stored in a retrieval system, or transmitted in any
form or by any means, electronic, mechanical,
photocopying, recording, or otherwise, without
express written permission of the publisher.

A note to readers: Names, locations, and identifying details of
some of the content portrayed in this book have been changed.

Published by LC Entertainment, Atlanta, Georgia
www.femalelikescheese.com

Edited and Designed by Girl Friday Productions
www.girlfridayproductions.com

Editorial: Amy Sullivan, Callie Stoker-Graham
Cover and Interior Design: Rachel Marek
Image Credits: cover © Barry J Holmes, leodaphne/
Shutterstock (sky), Meranda19/Shutterstock (paw prints)

ISBN (Paperback): 978-1-7344248-0-5
e-ISBN: 978-1-7344248-1-2
Library of Congress Control Number: 2020900373

First Edition

Printed in the United States of America

To my parents for loving and supporting me through all my adventures. To my family, to the few whom I can call kindred spirits, to Henry Hamilton for challenging me as a performer, to Rich Baker for being a sounding board professionally and personally, to PM for boating advice, and to my lobster, who may not fully measure up to Tom Hardy but is a close second . . .

Oh . . . and to Leonardo DiCaprio . . . because . . . well . . . Leo.

Ring Pops

I was out of breath and beaming. Everyone around me was shouting, "Yes! Yes!" Tommy had gotten down on one knee and asked me the million-dollar question—the one I had been hoping he would ask me all year long. I had spoken to all my friends about it. Imagined what this day would feel like or if it would ever come. My heart was pounding. I was sweating, which was a common occurrence for me. And when he slipped the blue Ring Pop on my finger and asked me to go out with him, I knew deep down we weren't really going to go anywhere. We were ten. Fifth grade was a hell of a year.

It was the fall of 1996 in Atlanta. The Braves lost to the Yankees after winning the World Series the year before. If you are an avid sports fans like me, you will agree that the Atlanta Braves had their best run in the nineties. Braves games were a big deal to me as a kid, not just because they were good then but because my dad took me to so many. I liked hanging with my dad, and we always had good seats. I really lucked out, and by lucked out, I mean that I didn't choose my parents, and they didn't choose me. We all kind of wound up in this ride of life together. See, I was adopted. Ten years prior to this pivotal time of deciding whether I was going to put on that blue Ring Pop, a confused nineteen-year-old girl was making an even tougher decision.

My biological mother met my biological father at the local A&P where they both worked. She was still in high school, and he was about seventeen years older. That must be where I get my attraction to silver foxes, but I digress. I can only imagine what they found attractive about each other. My father already had three children with his ex-wife, one who was only a few years older than my mother. My biological parents ended up moving in together, my mom got pregnant, it didn't work out, and they broke up. She was left with a tough choice and made the best decision for all involved. My father moved on to another younger woman, had two more kids, and stayed with her for a very long time. So to sum up, I have five biological sisters. I mean, for all the wives and girlfriends involved, this technically could be a Jerry Springer special. And my sisters, whom I've been fortunate enough to meet (it took me years to find them by stalking websites like Classmates.com), have joked about the hilarity of it all many decades later. However, that doesn't mean that there haven't been many repercussions from my biological parents' decisions that have affected my own upbringing. More on that later.

Tommy was probably boyfriend number one, if we would even call it that in the fifth grade. One thing I did have going for me with boys was that I was good at most sports. How this boy-crazy life all started, I'm not really sure, but if I had to guess, it would probably have been the daily kickball league known as recess. If you don't have kids in your life, or if you were the teacher's pet all of your childhood, then you may have forgotten that recess is one of the many big deals of elementary school. You knew before going to recess whom you'd be playing with that day, and if one of the cooler kids asked you to play with them, then unfortunately you'd have to cancel on Ginny. It's not every day you get asked to play kickball by the most popular girl in school. What Laura Perry brought to the table was a bunch of cute boys and the fact that she was really pretty. The intimidating thing about playing kickball was even though I could run fast, my catching skills were that of Scotty Smalls. Which made me feel like a complete and utter failure not just in front of the boys, but more importantly, in front of Laura Perry. Though she was the most popular, prettiest girl in school, she wasn't exactly the nicest. And that fucking bothered me. (That wasn't a word I used back then. I barely knew what the word *shit* meant. But if I knew what the word *fuck* meant, I probably would've mumbled it in my head a few times.) Why did the pretty ones have to be mean too? I mean, you already get to be pretty *and* popular. Is it so hard to be nice? I guess it made it easier to hate her. Side note: I ran into her a year ago at a mutual friend's wedding, after not seeing her in over ten years. It was interesting to observe the major role reversal. Her life hadn't turned out like I (or she, for that matter) had imagined, and instead of making some snarky comment about how she behaved back then with her arrogant attitude and trying to settle the score, I realized that she probably already went through the karma without someone like me reminding her of it. Plus, it's just not cool to do that in your thirties. She actually came up to me in a very shy way and asked how I was doing. Who knows, maybe we can play in an adult kickball league together one day.

Growing up in the suburbs of Atlanta in the nineties was bliss. It was everything you'd see in a movie. We lived on a cul-de-sac in a country club. I attended a private Christian school. I'd run around on the hot clay in the summer. (Careful of those hot rocks though. I hear they can damage a spring coat from Saks Fifth Avenue pretty badly.) I was spoiled as a child. Absolutely spoiled and sheltered, and I had no idea. My mom was heavily involved with the Baptist church in our town. I went to Bible summer camp, Sunday school, youth group, regular church service, chapel at school—you name it. It was actually a lot of fun. I remember Camp Power Time with a lot of my friends from Christian school. We were taught the normal things you learn in church: Save yourself for marriage. Be kind to others (Laura Perry needed to take notes). Remember the six-inch rule, which is not what you think! It means that when you are at a dance, you have to leave room between you and your date for Jesus. Jesus must be anorexic. Jesus needs a large fry from Chick-fil-A. But all that was normal to us. I didn't have many public-school friends in Atlanta. I only had friends from my school, my best friend, Sarah Anne (whom I had known since we were babies), and a couple of neighborhood friends from swim team, but I only hung out with them in the summer, and it was very supervised with sleepover rules. I remember the swim-team kids' parents let them do way more stuff than my parents. They were allowed to drink soda. I wasn't. I could only have "green Coke," a.k.a. Sprite, on vacation. They were allowed to listen to Ace of Base. I was allowed to listen to DC Talk and other Christian bands. But, in all honesty, life was good in Atlanta, and I had other things going on. Sarah Anne and I spent every Halloween together. She would get my hand-me-down costumes in the younger years, but I never noticed. We were too busy playing on the swings or riding bikes. Eating ice cream at Braves games or, for me, a naked dog. I was content. That's why, in the summer of 1999, when I had to part with my country-club boyfriend number umpteen, I was devastated. We were moving to south Florida. The world was ending. I don't even think my parents knew I had a boyfriend. (Unless Sarah Anne told her mom, who then told my mom, but that's beside the point now.) I didn't really tell them much. I mean, I was twelve. What am I going to talk to my parents about? I was a preteen, approaching the even more sullen years. No one consulted me on this decision. On spring break I was dragged from house to house with a real estate agent in the sweltering Florida heat. I hated the sand. It got in places that weren't friendly. But for some reason, I had a very indifferent attitude about moving. I have always been an outgoing person and enjoy meeting new people. I guess when I realized the move was really happening, I tried to see some positives in it. Of course, I never expressed any of this to my parents.

I never really talked to my parents about anything. They weren't approachable. I mean, my mother was all about rules and very strict. She was intimidating and came across as condescending at times. But other times she was the life of the party. It was very hard to gauge her. I could never figure out if I was going to get a no or a yes; usually it was a no. My dad was always steady. Even though he did have some rules, he usually had reasons behind them. I may not have understood the meaning behind a rule at the time, but I respected how he handled things. When I got to high school, this approach really helped. Sometimes I wonder if my parents were really strict because they had been through so much before I was even adopted. I don't have kids, so I can't imagine what it would be like having almost two adoptions go through and then the mother backing out. I definitely understand this position, but having parents born in the forties and still in the mindset of no one really talking about their feelings, I entered high school at a pivotal point when kids like me *needed* to talk about their feelings but had no resources to help them do it. So, I did what came naturally to me: sports, theater, and boys.

Me vs. High School

The one word that sums up high school for me: sheltered.

We had been in Florida a few years, and I actually had made some cool friends at my new private non-Christian school. Although my mom still made me go to the local church she had become a member of. I had some friends there, too, but they went to public school, thank God, and were really cool. Unlike my boyfriends in fifth and sixth grade, I was allowed to have an actual boyfriend, but that came with some major rules. My date options were limited to PG movies and high-school sporting events. Basically, anything the church deemed as OK. Parties were *not* on that list. Of course, I did go to a couple behind my parents' backs, which always involved sleeping over at the house of a friend who was allowed to go or parking my car in the movie theater parking lot and taking a friend's car. My parents put a GPS on my car and, strangely enough, told me about it. Why would you tell your kid about the GPS? All that does is create a good liar. I mean, I wasn't a bad kid. I didn't have my first sip of alcohol until senior year. It was a Budweiser, and I puked it up in the neighbors' bushes while my "very close guy friend" was taking me home from a "movie." I wasn't tempted to drink much before that, as I was a competitive athlete and I didn't want to ruin any chance of a scholarship. I just wanted to go to the parties to feel cool. I wanted to be at the watercooler the following Monday and know what everyone was talking about. I don't think parents realize how important it is just to be included in those conversations. If you even get invited to those parties at all. I was rarely lucky, but if I did go, I wasn't going to commit social suicide because my parents didn't understand what high school was like in the new millennium. Clearly things had changed since the sixties. They had no clue what we teens were up against.

But with my ninth-grade boyfriend at the time, we were just more interested in what movie we were going to see on a Friday night. Since he went to public school and had reasonable parents, he was allowed to see PG-13 movies. Before being driven to meet him,

I would have to go through the whole rundown with my mother on what movie we were seeing. There was a website parents in the congregation could browse called Plugged In, which broke down any content that could be deemed sinful in newly released movies (even for G and PG movies). For example, for sexual content, if two people were about to kiss, get it on, or whatever, they would have sentences like "Dressed in a revealing knit halter top." Oooh, knit! Scandalous! To this day, I still think this is outrageously funny. I can understand having rules about your kid not seeing an R-rated movie at fourteen or just being a morally good parent, but the website was overkill. Like your kid isn't already hearing shit-bombs in the halls of high school? Give me a break. And that was 2002! Now it's 2020—what kid hasn't seen *American Pie*? Actually, that movie is so old many teens probably haven't seen it—I'm sure it's considered a classic by now. And it wasn't just the movies—it was everything. My clothes were a problem, what time I could stay out (even though the state had a curfew)—everything was "No!" or just an extreme leash where I felt like I couldn't breathe. I didn't get punished or grounded a lot, because I was too afraid to try anything, but I think my all-time favorite punishment in high school was when my mom caught me and a boyfriend kissing on the couch in the living room and made me memorize a whole proverb from the Bible.

I lost my virginity my freshman year of high school. Which, in all honesty, even I will admit is too young. I even remember the exact date it happened. I loved him. Or whatever you call love in high school. The deed took place in the back seat of a car, which is so cliché. I didn't feel guilty for having sex, nor did I feel used. I never felt the emotions that some girls feel when they have sex for the first time. I knew at an early age I would lose my virginity before I was married. I am a very curious person, and I just knew there was no way I was waiting until my wedding night.

The rest of high school was tough, but only for me, of course—not for you heathens. Don't you know only one person suffers in high school, and that's me! Ha! I'm only kidding, we all suffer. I wasn't popular, but I did have friends. I was in drama club and ran track. I succeeded in both of those areas, and they made me happy, but I always felt like something was missing. Rejection was hard for me. I don't think I recognized rejection in all its forms at the time though. I mean, we all want to be liked. I think we just don't realize there is a difference between *wanting* to be liked and *expecting* to be liked. In high school, I think we all *expect* to be liked. The private school I went to set high expectations. This was great, academically. However, socially, it put a lot of pressure on me. Between my parents' social circle and the school, when I was let down or disappointed, I think the weight of it all was heightened. When this happened, of course I turned to boys instead of getting actual help from a professional. They found me funny. They found me cool. I wasn't trying too hard on the makeup. Hell, I didn't even know how to put it on, unlike some of the popular girls—I wish they would've taught me at their sleepovers I always heard about. They always looked so cute at the football games. But I was just me. Trying too hard to be me, when in reality I probably should've just been *me*. So I used the fact that I at least was skinny, liked sports, was funny, and didn't mind making out on a first date to be liked. My dad is a smart man. I wish I had just come to him for advice, but he wasn't really the type that I could talk to about this stuff. Whenever I asked him advice about a regular topic, he would always give me an option to do the right thing or to do what I wanted with the possibility of repercussions. It made me think about my choices rationally. I definitely wasn't going to talk to my mom, who eventually cornered me and questioned me about sex after reading my journal. I ended up throwing all my journals away, which is sad to think about now, because I had some really cool memories in there that had nothing to do with boys. As an adult, I share my journals, knowing people will somehow get ahold of them and nothing is private in this world anymore.

When I felt like I couldn't talk to anyone, I threw myself into theater. Most actors and comedians talk about how they once felt alone or different. We all are fucked up. There's no way around it. We've all had some form of trauma, but it's allowed us to be creative. Back in school, acting made me feel alive. Like many actors have said, throwing yourself into another part and becoming someone else allows you to forget about who you actually are. Umm, hello . . . that's me! I also used humor to distract myself from the feelings I was having about the boys I really liked not liking me back. What was wrong with me that made them not like me? Was I not pretty enough? Was I not skinny enough? Was I too loud? Too opinionated? It all probably stemmed back to feeling rejected by my biological parents. Why did they not want me? Why did they not love me enough to keep me? I was mean to the few boys I actually did like, probably because I projected this frustration onto them. However, the one that cheated on me—shame on you, Mark, I actually did like you—that just wasn't cool. Although, we were in high school, and hormones were flying. (You're still cute. Call me!) I started taking this rejection from my biological parents and searching for a fix. I needed to fill that void. That hurt. But where would I find it?

High school left a bad taste in my mouth. While kids were planning their homecoming and prom after-parties and creating never-forget, be-friends-forever memories, I felt like Rose from *Titanic* and was screaming inside. I couldn't wait to get out of high school, lock the door, and throw away the key. I knew college would bring my best years and a fresh start to fill that void.

Cool and The Gang

I specifically chose to go out of state for college, knowing that I needed to be far enough away that my mom couldn't jump in a car and show up in my dorm to spy on me. I know it seems like I'm dumping on my mom pretty harshly, but a lot of hurtful things happened in high school and continued throughout college. It was good I was going away for a while. I chose a school in North Carolina, because it was an easy nonstop flight home, just in case, and it had all the seasons. I figured it'd be a nice change of scenery from Florida, plus I was accepted on a theater scholarship. All that hating myself paid off. I didn't really know what I was doing when it came to socializing, as I had been to a total of two parties in high school. That became quite evident at the back-to-school bash at a local senior house. At this, my first real party, I quickly became known as *that* girl. You know her—the one who acts a fool, can't hold her alcohol.

Let's back up a second. How did I, a brand-new freshman, come to be at this senior party? It all began in the summer of 2005, when Facebook was in its infancy. The still-small social media site had only been in existence for about a year (shout-out to Mark Z.!), and it was very different than the Facebook we know today. Generation Z, I'm talking to you—these were the times when you had to have an official college email to create a Facebook account. I remember it felt like Christmas morning when the mail (yes, actual snail mail) arrived from the small liberal arts college I would be attending. In it was my roommate information, orientation details, and the most important thing of all . . . a college email address. I bolted fast, like I had the trots, to my new Dell computer with speedy dial-up and, priority number one, created my Facebook page (to this day I have never felt cooler in my life). I scrolled through all the profiles of my soon-to-be classmates (this was before the term *Facebook stalking* had entered the lexicon), and of course I scoped out the boys. I friended people like it was my job. I collected friends faster than others collect Instagram followers. (You know you care how many likes you get on your selfies, ladies, don't lie! It still takes me about eighteen tries to get a good one.)

One guy in particular caught my eye. For the sake of the book, any guy I talk about will be nicknamed, therefore, I'm going to call him Cool. He was a rising senior, so he was definitely way cool. So, Cool and I started messaging. This guy was practically out of a magazine. Ripped. Blond. Tan. Hoooooooottie McHot. He lived in Florida, too, so I thought *OK, this could work. We can carpool for Christmas break, summer break . . .* Florida is a big state, and we lived on opposite coasts, but obviously it didn't matter, because we were going to fall in love the first moment we met and would have a long-distance relationship until I joined him in whatever city he was living in, and I would get a job, and we would get married and have babies and live happily ever after. Duh. Quite the planner I was. We AIM'd (for those Gen Zers out there, that's instant messaging on our beloved dinosaur of AOL) and texted for most of the summer. We were looking forward to meeting each other at the annual back-to-school bash that his housemates threw every year. Now that they were seniors, this was going to be a big, exclusive, alcohol-filled rager. What a great way for me to start my college career, right? A freshie getting invited to a senior party! I was so excited, I wanted college to start immediately.

Orientation day finally arrived. There are few moments in life one cannot accurately explain to another unless they go through it themselves. I consider the day you go to college to be one of them—the feeling you get when stepping on campus, knowing this is your home for the next four years (or two for me, as I transferred midway), and the nerves, excitement, fear, and overwhelming emotions that go through your head and your gut. That first day of orientation, you wander around almost like you're afraid to say or do the wrong thing, but you don't realize that you're not the only one feeling the exact same thing.

My parents helped me move into my dorm. My dad unpacked all the electronics, while my mom sifted through my suitcases looking for any "scandalous" underwear. She, of course, threw the naughty ones out. But I, being smart, had some stashed away in a book bag, because who would snoop through a bag filled with actual books? After they finished moving me in, I ushered them out as quickly as I could and told them adios. I was free! Cue George Michael's "Freedom! '90" (Yes, this is what every kid of my generation sang in their head going to college.) I sat in my dorm room alone, reveling in my independence. For the first time, I was on my own. I was ready to embrace the world. But first, I had to figure out what to wear to this party that none of the other girls I met at orientation were invited to.

I settled on my Hollister jean skirt and a low-cut halter top (better than knit, I might add)—all very fashionable in those days. For the first time, I didn't have to hide a gym bag full of "risqué" clothes in the back of my car and change in a parking lot so my parents wouldn't see what I really wore. Cool picked me up at my dorm. That's right, not only was I a freshman attending a senior party (I know I keep repeating myself, but even I can't get over it), but I was also getting picked up and driven there like a damn princess. At the party, I got an education in drinking games. Flip cup, beer pong, kings, quarters—all of them. I remember kids in high school talking about these games and having no idea what they meant. Blow jobs, on the other hand . . .

Thanks to the strict rules my parents raised me with (you know, all that garbage I just talked about in the last chapter), I was like one of those cans that say they're full of nuts but snakes jump out when you open them. I was pent-up, full of desire to live life, and ready to explode. It was still considered summer in North Carolina, so it was quite muggy at nine p.m. Built in the twenties, the house was painted blue on the outside and resembled something you'd see in one of those murder shows on the Investigation Discovery channel. Cars were parked in the grassy makeshift driveway and all along the street as far as the eye could see. This didn't look like any party. This looked like *the* party. I remember walking in and noticing the house smelling like sex and an unpleasant brewery tour. There were couches everywhere, and what looked like a dining room was now empty, with a built-in wooden bar in one corner and the rest of the area cleared out as a dance floor. Scratched into the bar were names with numbers next to them, which I later found out were the "Shots of Fame." Each person that turned twenty-one wrote how many shots they did until they puked.

At this party, I drank alcohol like it was the end of times. I had beer, then wine, then shots, then back to wine. I didn't know the "beer before liquor makes you sicker" or "liquor before beer you're in the clear" rules. The music was poppin' (thanks, Akon's *Trouble* album), the alcohol was flowing (thanks, Hpnotiq and Mike's Hard Lemonade), and I was dancing the night away with Cool. There were so many people inside and tons of people outside. I was finally here. In college. Living it up.

Since I had no idea how much alcohol was too much (spoiler alert: it didn't take a lot), I drank way more than my body could handle. At some point early in the night, I officially became white-girl wasted (a term that wouldn't be coined for another few years). It got sloppy. So much so that—and I cringe having to write this next part—two nice senior girls took me upstairs to Cool's room, where I proceeded to pro-jectile vomit all over Cool's twin bed. My brain was mush. I had no idea what was going on. My guardian angels changed me into Cool's clothes. My memory of that night is a bit scattered (shocked?), but I do recall one of them saying to me "Oh, that's a cool tattoo." I had gotten a tattoo on my right upper ass cheek that summer before college, ~~because I didn't know where else to put it~~ because I didn't want my parents to see it. #winning

They cleaned me up and laid me facedown (because that's the safer position to be when sick with alcohol poisoning—college kids, take note) on Cool's bed. The next morning I would realize how uncomfortable that twin bed really was, but at the time I didn't seem to notice for some reason (read: alcohol poisoning). The girls stayed with me until Cool came to bed in his own drunken stupor. I was so grateful to those two seniors. They really were angels.

The next morning, I woke up with dried puke in my hair, desperately in need of a shower. Cool woke up, showed me the bathroom, and, well, one thing led to another, and we had some hungover morning sex. Honestly, all I could think of during it, besides my pounding headache and experiencing a *real* hangover for the first time (clearly two Budweisers was nothing like this beast), was *Who sleeps with a woman who just threw up in your bed?* Apparently that wasn't enough to turn off Cool. Lesson learned: it takes a lot more than a hangover and dried vomit to quell a college-age male's libido. Not my finest moment, but hey, I hooked up with a senior, so once again . . . #winning.

I then proceeded to go on my first walk of shame in his boxers and tank top. I was officially *that* girl. Whether or not any passersby noticed, *I* knew I was *that* girl. Eventually the story got out (it was a small school) and became a hard-earned lesson in pacing myself. A couple of days later, I asked around campus about the girls who took care of me, so I could apologize and thank them for what they did. They ended up becoming great friends of mine, and I even got to pay it forward later for others who experienced what I did. There were many nights spent at Senior House and with Cool that year. This was just the beginning.

Over the next few months, Cool and I continued to hang out. I attended a party every weekend at Senior House and became really good friends with the other guys in the house. It was no secret that I liked Cool, but after a few weeks and seeing what was out there, I figured it was best to keep my options open. I was single, and it was my first year of college. There were boys everywhere. On the weekends when they would throw a party, I would sleep over. Sometimes Cool and I would have sex, and sometimes I'd just crash there, because I didn't want to make my way back to the dorm. It was a very interesting relationship I had with Cool, and by no means normal. There was a lot of back and forth. I saw other people. He saw other people. I remember he went to winter formal with my friend Kathleen. I was so butt hurt because I wanted him to ask me. I had no idea why he *didn't* ask me. Once again, I was rejected by the guy that I thought liked me, and I was confused because there was no explanation. What had I done wrong? We had a wonderful time for six months. Did I not show him enough interest by seeing other people? Maybe that was my downfall too.

The rest of freshman year was a blur. I slept with a lot of people. Some of my favorites include the guy from the rodeo who wasn't a cowboy (I'd figure out how to rope one of those later in life) and a guy from high school I always liked and hoped would happen and finally did. I wish I could say I'm not proud of it, but I'm neither proud nor ashamed. It just was what it was. I think I had no idea who I was, so what was happening didn't really matter. Things were so new. Like that can of snakes I mentioned that pops out once the top is released. I was in college. Finally being accepted. Getting attention. Living my best life but having no idea what that actually meant. (Best life, by the way, does not equal sex. It equals mac and cheese and a nap and rosé—before everyone coined this "rosé all day" bullshit.)

Freshman year was coming to a close, and Cool and the gang were graduating and going their separate ways. It was hard parting with them, as some had become like brothers to me. They had had my back all year, and I had theirs in a way. I was sad there would be no more parties at Senior House. So much of my freshman year had been spent there—mostly on the couch toward the end, but still. It was my home, apart from my dorm room and randos' beds. (I even made it into a waterbed that year!) Cool and I promised to keep in touch. He would be in grad school not far. I would miss him, miss what could have been, and wonder why it hadn't worked out. But I was ready to get the hell out of Dodge and go home. The plan was to go to Europe that summer with Sarah Anne and—buzzkill—my parents. An adventure to get excited about. College life was definitely turning up, and my twenties were going to kick ass.

What The F*ck Was I Thinking?

I remember the day I met him so clearly. Sunday morning, May 17, I rolled out of bed, put on my cute red-and-white polka-dotted halter-top dress and white heels, and headed to the country club to meet my parents for Mother's Day brunch. I had barely been home a week from my first year of college. Besides saying goodbye to Cool and the gang, I had been dealing with the drama of sleeping with a guy for the last couple of months, until I got fed up with his *Van Wilder* "I'm still a twenty-six-year-old senior in college for the fourth time" bullshit and decided I was ready to have a fun summer. Europe was a month away, but in the meantime, fuck didn't have a face, and the possibilities were endless. I can't recall what I had done the night before, but my guess is I was nursing a hangover. I had gotten back in touch with the pool-hall crowd I used to hang with the summer before and figured that would be where my summer romances and shenanigans would come from. Wrong as usual. I still didn't understand the concept of "things don't go according to plan." I was dreading the brunch; family functions on my mother's side were not always my thing, as they could drone on and on at times, God love them. But on special occasions like Mother's Day, I knew I had to go forth with a good attitude and act like the daughter my dad had raised.

I pulled up to the valet and staggered out of my car. (We'll blame the heels.) I expected someone to greet me; isn't that their job? Hello—I may not be actual royalty, but I'm still a princess, damn it! Being naive but entitled at the same time, I was a little confused when Jesse Pinkman (I'll call him this because let's just say he really, really liked *Breaking Bad*—on many levels) came out with the valet guy. He was wearing a navy jacket and khaki slacks, just like you'd see at most conservative country clubs. He had short brown hair, shiny loafers, a nice watch. Everything that shouted "I worked my ass off to get in this position, and no one is going to take it away from me or stop me from climbing this ladder." He escorted me through the lobby, making small talk. "So, you must be

Mr. Member's daughter?" Of course, not knowing who he was, I replied, "Yeah, how'd you know?" I thought, *Who is this guy? Can you just fuck off? I'm late, and I need to find my dad.* He continued with more questions, and I mentioned that I had just returned home from college. We walked into the main dining room, and as we approached my family's table, he said, "Well, I hope you have a good summer." He then walked over to speak with other members. I sat down and said my hellos with my happy face on, wishing I was anywhere but there. It was sunny out. I had been home for two days. I wanted pool time and a cocktail in my hand. It was very bright in the room, and that was not helping my mental state. What did help was checking him out from across the room. I couldn't help but notice he was attractive as he was tending to other members. And I couldn't stop staring at him, wondering if he had a girl-friend or whether he could be my fun summer fling. I kept trying to guess how old he was. Finally, I excused myself to go to the bathroom. On the way, I bumped into him, on purpose, only to find out that he was the food and beverage manager. We got to talking about summer break and college, typical awkward small talk to feel someone out. He had a recommendation for me on something I don't remember, so I gave him my num-ber, went to the ladies' room, and then sat back down with my parents, pleased with my accomplishment.

Back then, the book *The Rules* was still very pop-ular. This whole "wait three days before a guy will call you" bullshit was a big deal, so I wasn't expecting a call right away. After brunch, we came home, and I decided to take a nap, because that is always a highlight of my day, and just as I was about to doze off, my trendy flip phone started flashing. The number scrolled across the tiny screen, and I flipped it open, because that's how it worked.

Me: "Hello?"

JP: "Hey, Lauren. It's Jesse Pinkman."

Internally freaking out and doing a happy dance while lying down, I replied:

Me: "Oh hey. What's up?"

He had called to tell me about that thing he was recommending (which was nothing I couldn't have found on my own). I thanked him, and toward the end of the call said:

Me: "We should hang out sometime."

JP: "Yeah, that'd be cool."

OMG, I guess he is single. Me, trying to be very cool:

Me: "All right, I'll catch ya later."

JP: "OK, bye."

Ending the call, I was very satisfied at how it all went down. But then I started second-guessing myself. *I'll catch ya later?* Like when? There was no plan. I'd just left it to the universe to decide. That could be never. *Maybe he'll call. We'll hang out. This will happen.* A day went by. Then two. No calls. I started to question everything, like one does at nineteen. I still didn't know much about him. Remember: this was before Instagram. Facebook had been around only two years, so no stalking could be had without a last name or college email. If you were really going to stalk someone, you had a better chance at cozying up to their ex to get the deets or perusing their Myspace. I had to rely on fate. By the third day, I was antsy as fuck. *Why had this guy not called me? Maybe he does have a girlfriend. Maybe he isn't interested. Maybe my game is off. Maybe sleeping with Van Wilder for two months killed it, and I need to find someone to break the spell.* I also thought, *Well, this is ridiculous. Don't we live in the age where women can make the move and ask a guy out? What's the harm? He can say no.* Deep down I don't know if I would've been able to handle him saying no. I wasn't secure at that age. I wasn't as grown-up as I thought I was. But I was going to do it anyway, because I thought I knew it all. I think being a little naive and knowing nothing about myself internally helped at that moment in time. I held my breath while the phone rang. I heard a fart slip out; I was so nervous my stomach was in knots. *How do guys do this? Answering machine, thank God. Fuck, what do I say?* I hadn't rehearsed that part. I usually rehearsed everything in the mirror, in the shower, in the car. I was doing that long before Issa Rae made it a thing on *Insecure*.

"Hey, Jesse Pinkman. It's Lauren. I was just calling to see what you were up to this week and if you wanted to grab a bite." I couldn't actually say *drinks* because I was underage. "Let me know. Bye."

I hung up the phone and sweated as I paced back and forth in my room. *Why would any woman want to do this? This is not meant for us at all.* I threw my phone down and went outside to get some air. About thirty minutes later, I came back upstairs and saw I had a missed call from him. When I returned his call, he asked me if I wanted to grab dinner that night at a wine bar (so sophisticated). I said, "Yeah, that sounds great. Do I need to get a fake ID?" I felt like such a child. I was so embarrassed. He told me it wouldn't be an issue, whatever that meant. When we got off the phone, I was jumping up and down with excitement. A real date. With an adult. Not some college guy. This was with an *adult* who had a *real* job. He didn't work at Starbucks or the school bookstore. I was used to telling my parents half-truths about my social activities, so I said I was going to have dinner with a friend. Which was kind of true. I tried on, like, eight outfits before deciding on the worst thing ever. It was summer in Florida. Sweltering heat. And I decided to wear black pants and a coral top and heels. First of all, that's not fashion. That shit didn't match. The pants were great because they accented my ass, but I had no boobs at that time. And no fashion game, clearly. Did I not learn from my mother the one thing she's good at? Fashion? The night before, I had been over at a friend's house in the north county, and we decided to dye parts of our hair for fun (it was the trend). Some of the streaks hadn't washed out all the way, so I had one streak of blue still remaining. If you don't already know this, blue fades to gray. I had a streak of gray. I was totally not fashionable at all, but I was clueless and excited for my date.

We met at a wine bar in town. I was nervous and sweaty. I didn't want him to accidently touch my hands. (A reoccurring theme—who wants to hold hands with a catfish?) The wine bar was small and quaint, and Jesse Pinkman knew the owners. It was a very sophisticated place, and I was going to act appropriately. We weren't doing Jell-O shots and ordering amaretto sours. We sat down for dinner and split some apps. I had duck confit for the first time. Though I had eaten many different meals in many different countries, I had never tried duck before, and it was delicious. He asked me about school, and I tried very hard to be as grown-up as possible and not act like the huge partier that I was, and he told me about his adventures skydiving and traveling. I eventually asked about his living situation. He mentioned that he was still living with his ex-girlfriend, because they owned their townhome together, but he was about to move out. It was strictly a financial thing, and there was nothing between them anymore. I wasn't exactly thrilled at this answer, but the fact he was going to be moving in with a friend soon made me think that if this went somewhere, we were off to a good start. Some people would think this was a red flag, but at nineteen, I believed Jesse Pinkman, because he had a job and had his shit together. There was no need to be lying to anyone. Especially since he worked at the country club where my family were members, and we would be seeing him so often. After dinner, he suggested we go for a walk on the beach. I wasn't going to admit I hated the beach. To everyone else in the world, it is considered a romantic destination, but not to me. I would let the sand win, but only this once. The moon was shining bright. It was a very beautiful, breezy evening. We held hands. We sat down and talked some more. And then, finally, as he leaned in for a kiss, I uttered the romantic words, "Don't fuck this up." Insert the face-palm emoji that hadn't been invented yet here. Why I would say something stupid like that, I don't know. But he just smiled and kissed me anyway. The kiss was OK. As far as technique goes, it wasn't out of this world, but the moment was romantic. As I lay in bed that night, I felt butterflies. I had a crush. Unlike with college boys, I had a big-girl crush—an adult crush—and I hoped he would ask me out again soon.

We became "official" the summer of 2006. I was seeing him regularly, and by regularly, I mean a few times a week. I was living at home that summer, and my dad had given me the option to focus on my golf game instead of getting a job, so that was keeping me busy during the day. In the evenings, when Jesse Pinkman wasn't working, we would go out to a comedy show or to dinner or down to Fort Lauderdale to visit his friends and do things that I considered to be *super* adult. I had to lie to my parents *a lot*. I tried to be honest at first and tell them he was hanging out with us in a group. Dad didn't like it, but who was he to tell me who I could and couldn't hang out with? I was nineteen. I was an adult. I could make my own decisions. I was invincible.

The first year was magical as we fell in love. Even though I had gone back up to college in North Carolina, we made the distance thing work. I remember saying goodbye to him after our amazing summer together. I was crying, he was crying. It was going to be so tough to not be around him. And for him too— or so I thought at the time. We had a plan already mapped out for me to fly home in a month to see him. I wouldn't tell my parents, and he would buy my plane ticket. This worked out a few times, but after hiding our relationship for the better part of a year, I had to come clean. My parents were not at all happy. They didn't like Jesse Pinkman and for good reason. He had a past. He had made some mistakes that a lot of college kids make when they're young and stupid. "He fought the law, and the law won" type of thing. They also didn't like that he was about ten years older than me and that he worked at the country club. Country-club relation-ships define your social status. If someone is dating the help, it can get very awkward for members. They threatened to take my car away at school, threatened to get him fired from the club. I didn't see any of this at the time, because I was young, and we were in love, and we were going to be together. Eventually my par-ents realized there was nothing they could do. He had come clean about his past to me, and I had accepted it, because he swore he had changed. I was looking to our future.

For Worse or for Worse

The next couple of years were a roller coaster of adventure. Despite my parents' disapproval, he took me so many places. I went to Napa Valley for the first time and experienced an environment that to this day I still appreciate. I remember being nervous going to my first winery. I was still underage at the time, only twenty, but he knew many winemakers, and I was able to do tastings no questions asked. I knew nothing about wine then, let alone the sophisticated winemakers, and I didn't want to sound stupid, so I simply listened and observed. I wanted to soak everything in. Once I turned twenty-one, he took me to Vegas, introduced me to Cirque du Soleil, and whisked me around to all the hotels. We drove to the Grand Canyon. I felt like I was on a high with him. Once I got back to school, I remember sitting in class, and while everyone was discussing their trips to shitty beach towns, I was boasting about how I went on sophisticated adventures with my older boyfriend. I felt so much cooler than other people. Or so I thought . . .

Everything wasn't perfect, despite our grandiose adventures. We did have our fights. Sometimes he would shout at me. Or sometimes he would make me feel like a dog that peed on the floor. I felt a lot of times things were my fault for no reason. Maybe I had done something wrong? I wasn't really sure. Lots of confusion. But I know some of the issues were over trust. He didn't seem to tell the whole truth about situations, which led to me questioning him about places he'd go or people he was with. Time and again he reassured me that there was nothing to worry about. Right before my final semester, we got into a huge fight over his ex-girlfriend, with whom he was still friends. There was yelling involved. I just wasn't comfortable with it. If we were eventually going to spend our lives together, I thought starting fresh and living our own life was best. I was going to be graduating in the fall, and I knew I wanted to marry him, but I couldn't marry someone that wasn't going to put me first. Eventually he told her they couldn't be friends, and that was the proof I needed to move forward and be all in with this relationship. All my worries were finally pushed to the side.

He proposed in late October 2009. We had just been to a family friend's wedding and had driven up to Orlando for the rest of the weekend. This was his idea, of course, saying it would be a fun thing to do before I went back for class the following week. He suggested we go to SeaWorld and maybe see a show. SeaWorld is where we had our first getaway weekend when we started dating three years prior. Earlier in the week, I had said to a friend, "I bet you I'll be engaged when I come back to class." She reminded me that I had said this before, which I had, but something in my gut told me that now was the time. It's very hard to hide things from me. My gut is always right. On that Sunday, we spent the day at SeaWorld, seeing the exhibits, riding the rides, and toward the end of the day, we headed to the penguin exhibit. Penguins are one of my favorite animals. If it were allowed, I would have one as a pet in a heartbeat. Jesse Pinkman had arranged to meet a king penguin during our tour. This beautiful bird came out all handsome, and there, in front of fifteen people, Jesse Pinkman kneeled down and asked me to marry him, with the penguin standing astutely by his side. I said yes, of course. Would you say no? I bet the penguin would've bit me if I said no. A random woman on the tour had her video camera out and happened to get the whole scene on camera. She said she would email it to us but never did.

I was over the moon. The ring was beautiful—a princess-cut diamond with trillions on the side, totaling two and a half carats. Perfect for my pudgy knuckles. (No matter how skinny or fat I get, my knuckles don't change—they haven't since I came out of the womb. They remain a constant fat. I will never be a hand model like Joey Tribbiani.) We drove south to see my parents for a celebratory dinner, which my parents seemed excited about, or so they played the part, then I drove back to school the following day so I could shove the ring into my friend's hand and say "See!" with an I-told-you-so look. I was getting married to the man I was so in love with, and I could not wait!

I dove right in to wedding planning. I knew already where I wanted to get married—The Breakers in Palm Beach. It was such a magical place, and I had dreamt of having my wedding there since moving to south Florida. It was a palace on the beach. Celebrities were married there, foreign princesses—friends that I knew had attended weddings there. This was my dream wedding, and I set the date for May. It wouldn't be too hot, so we could have it outside by the sea. Not on the beach. I definitely did not want it on the beach. I hate sand. (I can't say this enough!) And I had to have the reception in the big ballroom facing the ocean. All the bells and whistles!

When the day finally arrived, I was very anxious but tried to stay calm. I wanted everything to be perfect. My eight (yes, eight) bridesmaids all wore royal blue dresses and held pink bouquets. I wore a white satin dress by Ulla Maija. Because that is all important for being written up in a bridal magazine. Three hundred guests attended and danced to an amazing fifteen-piece band during the reception. Tables were set with three different arrangements, one even resembling a spiral staircase (to heaven?). And the food—that I didn't get to eat—I *heard* was incredible. We had a buffet that was bigger than the one at Bellagio in Vegas. There was sushi, mac and cheese, steak, lamb, a dessert bar, and an actual martini glass of ice cream served individually. Hell, after seeing the wedding video, I wanted to attend my own wedding. I remember waiting to walk out with my dad. There were so many people around, and I was nervous. Dad and I never had a moment. There was no exchange. I wanted him to walk and focus. Everything needed to be on point. This was like a production. It felt like my job. Walking down the aisle in front of all the people, I didn't cry. Jesse Pinkman didn't cry. I looked at him when I reached the altar. My nerves were still a mess, but we were both smiling. I was happy that I was getting the fairy-tale ending. We spent most of the wedding reception apart, talking to everyone and saying our thank-yous. I danced up a storm with my friends. It was the party of the year.

Looking back, I will never forget that day. I am very appreciative of my dad, who paid for the amazing event. I was fortunate to have my dream wedding. But unfortunately, I didn't get my dream marriage.

I Hear a Leak

Our first year of marriage was a breeze. Since we already lived together, we were in a routine for the most part. He was still working at the country club, and I was trying to find production jobs in the film industry. There were a few opportunities in south Florida, but if something came about in New York or Los Angeles, I'd take it on location. I didn't take many, though, as I was newly married, and I figured I would enjoy wedded bliss before diving into being a working woman. We spent time doing couple things: we hung out with our neighbors, we took weekend trips to the Keys. We had amazing dinner parties at Ruth's Chris with copious amounts of wine. We were happy. When I was sick, he'd go out of his way to pick up medication at the pharmacy for me. When I knew he had had a big week working over sixty hours at the club and needed a relaxing day off, I would book him a massage at a spa. We'd take the dog on walks around the neighborhood before making dinner together and binge-watching *Breaking Bad* (you know, Jesse's favorite) with a bottle of wine. All of his years in the food and beverage industry meant he really knew how to make some amazing dishes from scratch. One time he made me chicken potpie and left out the peas because he knew I hated them. When we were out with friends and one of us was ready to leave, we could let the other one know with just a look. I felt as if we were a team.

And then . . . there was a crack in the boat, and it started to leak two years in. Lots of excuses. Lots of white lies. Lots of high-pitched yelling. Lots of storytelling and confusion. I put a lot of the blame on me. Maybe it was my fault? I tried to fix me. There had been cutbacks at his job, so he had resigned, and I pinpoint that as the start of the demise. There was also a girl from the spa and country club we were members of (not the one he worked at) who kept hanging around. Something didn't seem right with that situation. She kept popping up at birthday dinners and Christmas parties. I told a friend that I didn't trust her and his behavior around her wasn't appropriate. He was always flirting with her, and not the innocent office flirting, but the "you've had too much to drink and you grabbed her ass" type flirting. The year and a half that followed was chaotic at best. He was making choices that were hurting the marriage and putting me in a very tough position emotionally and physically. I couldn't take the pain from his actions anymore. I mean, how cliché is it that he left me for the country-club babysitter, and we didn't even have kids? As fun as it would be to go into the nitty-gritty details of every single lie, argument, cheating scandal, and possible illegal incident, that would be another book in itself, and I don't want to waste too much time on Jesse Pinkman. He's just not worth it.

In June of 2014, I filed for divorce. It was a soul-crushing event. I was twenty-seven years old. I had only been married four years. You don't expect to be going through a divorce at such an early age. I filed and flew off to meet my dad in Spain. He was already over there for a golf trip and suggested I get away for a couple of weeks. We spent two weeks doing low-key sightseeing. I was so emotionally drained that just getting out of the hotel and going to a museum was a big deal for me. There was a lot of drinking, but it was good to spend some quality time with my dad. He really is my best friend. I questioned why I had pushed him away so much toward the end of my marriage, but looking back it makes sense. I was going through so much emotionally—I had been pushing everyone away. He was that steady rock with the reasonable advice, and I just wasn't ready to hear that yet. Just like when I was a teenager. I remember one night we were at a rooftop bar in Seville. He was delicately reassuring me that one day down the road I would find someone again, but I tuned that out. For the first time in my life, I wasn't boy crazy. I wasn't boy *anything*. And here my dad was trying to promote it. Good for him. Seeing the positives in love. Go, Dad!

Returning from Spain and realizing I was going to be venturing off into the single world again made me feel very alone. I read many divorce articles and remember one of them talking about all the feelings you have when you get divorced, including random breakdowns—of which I had a few. I think my favorite one was at a very popular bar on the water, jamming out to a great band, then cut to me seconds later sobbing next to a million-dollar yacht, wailing into my big-boobed friend's chest over and over that I shouldn't be allowed in public. Another one was trying my hardest to sleep in the middle of the bed—because fuck it, I could—but continuing to roll to the side that was mine for so many years. Adjusting to these things was going to take some time. I was questioning myself. This idea of being twenty-seven and divorced was still haunting me. Was anyone going to date me? Divorce is so common, but I was so young. I felt like I would be judged.

I spent a month on the couch drinking white wine like it was water. I was watching *all* the shows on Investigation Discovery, and by all, I mean I could tell you if it was a rerun, what time it came on, if the actors starred in other Investigation Discovery channel shows—the list goes on. My favorite was *Southern*

Fried Homicide, and you can never go wrong with *Forensic Files*. When in doubt, it's always the husband that kills the wife over the life insurance policy. I mean, that's Detective 101. My healing process consisted of me waking up, realizing the miserably shitty life I was living, crying, going to the fridge, opening a bottle of wine, eating leftovers (mostly pasta or anything that would make me fat), watching TV, passing out, eating more leftovers, watching more TV, drinking more wine, nap number two, having a friend call and check on me to make sure I was alive and not puking in a toilet. On a good day, maybe I'd throw on workout clothes and brush my teeth and meet my parents at dinner somewhere sans makeup. But that was a good day. Eight years of my life had just been ripped from me. I was beyond consolable. I was numb. I didn't care if I lived or died. I was just trying to breathe through the days.

D ...
Is not for Dick
... Sadly

Nothing prepares you for the day you get divorced. D-Day. I remember waking up and feeling anxious as I was getting ready. I tried to mentally tell myself it was going to be OK if I was sad or happy or if I cried. I had never been in a courtroom before. The hearing was set for early in the morning. I remember wearing a blue polka-dotted dress and sweater—I figured just in case it was cold and my sweaty hands needed a break? Knowing me, though, I'd probably be gripping my dress with them, hoping I wouldn't have to shake anyone's hand. My attorney and I sat in in a small room within the courtroom with a bunch of other divorcées. I felt like Ross Geller should've been there. In the state of Florida, only one party has to appear, and of course Jesse Pinkman wasn't going to show his face. He didn't even have the balls to move his stuff out of our house; I had to do it with the movers. (*Cough*—pussy.) My attorney tried to make light of the situation by cracking jokes about some of the *Real Housewives*–looking characters, but nothing was going to make me feel better about the scarlet letter *D* I was going to be carrying after that day. Once it was my turn, my dry mouth was able to utter the words while my right hand was raised, and it was over and done within a few minutes. It took longer to get married than divorced. As the judge stamped the divorce decree, it felt like the sound of judgement could be heard around the world.

I left the courthouse feeling very confused. For the first time in a while, I truly had no idea what to do. I got in the car and decided to just drive. I got on the freeway and ended up driving to The Breakers, where it all began. I don't know what possessed me to do that. In all honesty, I don't remember driving there from the courthouse. I just remember getting out at the hotel and telling the valet I was there for lunch. It's very eerie looking back. It feels like an out-of-body experience. I guess a part of me wanted closure. I wanted to relive my marriage one last time before truly leaving it behind, although I don't think something like that ever leaves you for good. I walked the halls and admired things about the hotel I hadn't noticed in a while, like the tall ceilings and big chandeliers. I sat down at the restaurant and ordered a glass of champagne and stone crab claws. I ate in silence, not looking at my phone once. I just sat and imagined our wedding. Imagined how happy I was that day and the smiling faces in the room. I also felt some relief, too, like I got a part of me back, even though I didn't know which part of me that was or who exactly I was. I just felt like *something* was back inside of me. Even though I didn't know what my plan was yet, I did feel a sense of closure—that the last two years of manipulation, lying, and sneaking around bullshit I had been put through were over.

I left the hotel and drove away, knowing one day I'd be back, but not for a long time. Not until I was ready. And then, about halfway home, the tears came rushing down. I was overwhelmed by so many feelings. I knew that this was a start to something new. I don't think I understood at the time that it was OK for me to feel these feelings. I hadn't learned the art of processing yet. I was still very good at the "push it all down inside" method.

When I got home, I was a little unsure of what to do with myself. Not going to lie—I was a little uncontrollable emotionally. I wasn't crying—I was just feeling very weird. *Overwhelmed* I guess would be the word. So, impulsively, I jumped in the pool with my wedding dress on. I gave no fucks. I popped a bottle of champagne, smoked some cigarettes (I don't usually smoke), and floated around with a pool noodle for a bit. If I was going down, that gown was going down with me that day. It was invigorating. Later that evening, I went out with my parents and some friends to celebrate with a little divorce party. I had a few too many margaritas, then went home and passed out. My dress spent the night on the lounge chair by the pool.

Looking back, my parents weren't overly vocal about my divorce in a negative or positive way. It wasn't like "OMG, thank God you're getting a divorce!" or "Oh no, you're getting a divorce?" They were supportive. I didn't like crying in front of them. It was uncomfortable, but it happened, and they understood. At first, they didn't tell me they thought he was a jerk, but as time moved on and I was able to say he was an asshole, then they did. They knew he wasn't exactly right in the head. When I was finally able to acknowledge all the terrible things that had happened, feelings from family and friends came out of the woodwork. Sarah Anne, who never liked him but had kept her mouth shut, spoke her truth. The fact that everyone had seen this but me kind of sucked. It helped me feel less crazy though. It helped me feel validated. It was a relief to know I wasn't going to have to make any more excuses for his behavior to the people I cared about. It was finally over. I had learned many lessons and had many more to go. There was a lot of pain to recover from, and it was going to be a long road ahead, but I figured there was no need to start this anytime soon.

Kansas and The Firepit

I had lost my dog to my ex. I was a mess. I thought this man was going to be by my side the rest of my life, and I had also lost some close friends. I was on the down-and-down. I had gained a lot of weight. Not the kind of weight you gain when you tell your friend "OMG, Kelly, I, like, put on five pounds this summer because of all the partying I've been doing at the roof-top bars," but real weight . . . depression weight. If any of you have suffered from depression, you know what it's like, this type of weight. The weight that makes you feel totally inadequate. The weight that makes you say,

Hey, I might as well keep eating because it doesn't matter anymore. I was inconsolable during that summer.

I've always had bouts of depression throughout my life. Some people understand depression, others *think* they understand depression, and then there is a handful that wants nothing to do with mental health whatsoever. Which is disappointing. It is a real thing, and whether it is depression or another mental health issue, it can completely take over you at times. But, moving on . . . I still wasn't completely out of my trash TV and alcohol phase, but I had switched to vodka, at least. Which, let's be real, just hides the fact that you're an alcoholic. I wasn't really talking to anyone about my problems. My therapist, whom I had been seeing for about eight years, wasn't really helping me. I felt like we were just in a stagnant place. My mom tried to take me to fat camp. Yes, fat camp. When your mother says the reason why you're not happy is because you're fat, there comes a point where you really don't know whether to laugh, cry, or drink. I think I did all three. The reason why I wasn't happy was because I was going through a divorce, and my life was unraveling. I was not only unhappy but also fat, so I guess there was some truth to that. The world, at least in my eyes, was ending, so I gave fat camp a try. It wasn't technically fat camp but a weight-loss and wellness place similar to Canyon Ranch. I lasted four days (with my mother). I did lose six pounds there, but that's beside the point. It wasn't the exercise that I minded as much as it was the food. I'm fine eating healthy, but no salt, no oil, no sugar—no fun. I don't like salt added on my food, but no fruit? No olive oil? Give me a break. I'd rather work out twice a day and eat a bowl full of fruit than go back to that prison. It was just what I needed to get myself back to reality.

When I got home and was enjoying just one serving of whole wheat pasta (one good thing I learned from fat camp) while cleaning the kitchen, I walked by a pair of boxing gloves. Boxing was something I had always been interested in. Watching it on TV and having some friends that had done it professionally, I figured I would take the plunge and put this "body after breakup" and "fuck it" list into motion. My "fuck it" list consisted of things I wanted to do or try since the divorce, such as the following: a new sport (boxing), Neuschwanstein Castle (and Euro adventure), Japan, Indian food, build a firepit, dress up like Wicked Witch of the West, go to US Open, go to Barcelona vs. Madrid, and the list goes on.

There was only one boxing club that was for fitness in our area. I walked into the afternoon classes knowing that I was going to be a little out of my element, but I'm not afraid of a challenge. I'm an outgoing person—please, God, I hope you all know this by now—and being sports savvy, I knew that I would catch on quickly. The guy teaching the class, Kansas, was very attractive. Ladies, you know how in yoga when you have to do the sun god pose? Well, let's just say he was what you would hope a sun god looked like. With sweat glistening down the side of his face, it was almost as if the ceiling parted and angels started singing as he stood over you telling you, "Ten more!" as you got down for ab rounds between punches. This guy was exciting. He was energetic. He was . . . constantly checking on me during class to make sure my form was correct, since I was new, and let's face it—I was totally OK with the attention. After class I signed up for a one-year membership and became addicted, not just because I loved the workouts but also because of the hot trainer.

I started coming to class three times a week, initially taking only Kansas's classes, but not wanting to look obvious when I really started crushing on him, I had to mix it up. I mean, this is Crushing 101. This was my first crush out of the gate postdivorce, so exactly what you think would happen, happened. Kansas became my rebound guy. I would make any excuse to linger after class (which, looking back, just made me look desperate), but then sometimes I would switch it up and leave. I mean, it was a game. I was trying to figure out if he was interested or not. It was exhausting. After talking after class for a few weeks, I happened to mention a home improvement project I had been thinking of working on. Being the good listener (stalker?) that I was, I knew he just happened to be interested in home improvements, as he did many of his own. I figured that would be a great way to get to know each other better and for him to fall completely in love with me, of course. Duh. Now I had a reason to cross something off my "fuck it" list. I love sitting outside and having a glass of wine and listening to music by a fire. I wasn't really sure how I was going to accomplish this task on my own, but recruiting a fine gentleman like Kansas would be a good start. So, he agreed to my firepit project, and after gathering supplies at Home Depot, he came over, and I quote to you from my journal, I kid you not:

> So today he shows up, and we are in the backyard digging the hole, and he takes his shirt off. WTF! His body is a wonderland! I mean sweat is just glistening down his torso. #porn So I had to change the subject somehow and shut my gaping mouth, so like an idiot I say, "Oh, look, a callus on my hand," and he says, "Those on a woman are sexy." FML.

Ladies and gentleman, do you want to know what I did that day? Something *so* adult and *so* mature: I pushed him into the dirt. I pushed that beautiful body into the fucking dirt. I couldn't take it. I was like a schoolkid on a playground. (I mean, how did Tommy with the Ring Pop even date me?) Because that is the type of tantrum this lady used to throw. Kansas took it as flirting. I took it as frustration, because I couldn't tell a boy I liked him at the time. So, ladies, when in doubt, I guess just push him in the dirt. I was terrible at flirting. I had been with someone for eight years, so my flirting muscles were very rusty. If this was my idea of flirting, I wonder what my idea of sex was!

This whole awkward flirting game went on for a few more weeks. Kansas would come over, and we'd dig more holes (to bury my dignity in) or set stones—I don't fucking know. I thought rebound guys were supposed to be fun, casual things, but this wasn't fun at all. This was like homework in school. Every day I'd come home from "class," and I'd strategize on what I needed to do to make better "grades." If I had actually spent half the time in real school that I spent on Kansas, I would've had a 4.0. I was having to chase him, but I almost didn't know what race I was running. After all, I hadn't dated since 1884. He wasn't exactly telling me he wasn't interested, but I was confused, so I figured if the firepit thing didn't work, then I'd write him a poem. . . . Like a moron.

Middle School

When Monday's got you feeling blue,
here is what you ought to do.

Sometimes it's slim pickins, we should
just stop acting like chickens.

Finding one that you like, is not as easy
as riding a bike.

When a girl likes you, and working in
the yard makes her look like poo,

You should ask her on a date so she can
throw on something great.

Camping counts, too, I want to see
those springs they call blue.

I can wear something schmancy, if you
want to go fancy.

Come out whenever, that doesn't mean
forever.

We both like our space, so you can stay
at your place.

Let's take a chance, as Lady Gaga says,
a "Bad Romance."

I wouldn't miss out, to go down the
route,

So man up as you say, because I may
take your breath away.

I could be out of line,

but as Bill Engvall says, "Here's your
sign."

OK, did everyone make it through that in one piece? I think I peed a little out of embarrassment, but I'm OK, I changed my pants. I know what you're thinking: First, that's a very good poem—fuck yes, it is. (He never mentioned how good of a poem it was after I gave it to him—sheesh!) And second, the divorce made me a little crazy. But in my defense, was I? Because the things he was saying and doing did not add up to rejection. Oh no. Flirty texts. Going on boat rides with my parents to dinner. These are things that boyfriends do, people! Or like *really* good friends. Not some dude that comes over to my punching bag during class and flirts and then swings by my house on the weekends and drinks scotch and digs holes (that I need to go live in out of embarrassment) but doesn't make a move. At this point, I was so confused. I couldn't stop questioning myself. Is he gay? Am I ugly? Look, I know I'm not Olivia Wilde, but I'm not Oscar Wilde either!

Kansas asked me to take him to the airport on Christmas Eve, and then finally a few days before New

Year's Eve, I purged my feelings out. I couldn't take it anymore. I had said stuff before, but this was the big finish. I am one for a good dramatic ending.

Looking back, I think two things were happening here: One, I just wanted an excuse to spend more time with him, hoping that he would like me. That it would *make* him like me. That somehow he would think, *Oh, look how cool and fun she is*, and boom, we're in a relationship. And two, I wanted my old marriage back. I didn't necessarily want my ex back, but I wanted what we *had* back. Change was ready for me, but I wasn't ready for it. I had spent so much time trying to get Kansas to like me, because I didn't like me very much. I didn't like that I was alone (and this coming from someone who likes being independent). I didn't like that someone had done me wrong. (Hey, Dr. Phil, it's ya girl.) I especially didn't like that I had no idea who the hell I was and felt as if I were behind everyone else in figuring it out. I hadn't yet realized that these feelings were normal to have. It was my first Christmas in eight years without someone. If you're not drunk, high, or pulling an Anne Hathaway type of scenario like in *Rachel Getting Married*, then props to you. Even though I was foolish and stupid, I don't regret it. I had to go through it to learn from it. I ended up giving up on Kansas. He wasn't interested and made it clear after I professed my love at New Year's. So I distanced myself from him and continued working out at other times, minding my own business. I wasn't going to quit something I loved just because I got rejected by a boy. I at least learned that in my twenties. You should never quit doing something you enjoy because of an awkward situation. But that lesson you learn in elementary school about ignoring boys so they end up liking you? Funny how that works out.

I was giving Kansas no attention, and then one day, months later, things shifted. All of a sudden he wanted to get together. It was the tail end of spring breakers in town, and to be honest, I just didn't feel like going out. I had had a big week, and I was exhausted. I told him he was welcome to come over and have some tacos, but I wasn't in the mood to get dolled up. (Who is this person?) We sat outside, had tacos, lit a fire, and caught up, just like old friends would. I guess I was allowing for some closure here, until he started apologizing. Apologizing because he didn't know how he felt and he didn't handle things in the best way and "you really are beautiful" and "I really am attracted to you." So the flirting commenced. The scotch was had. There was slow dancing, I think? (I mean, can someone help me out of the giant embarrassment that I'm drowning in? Oh look, the pool we're dancing next to . . . I can just drown in that.) So we came inside, and we got aggressive on the granite and rounded a few bases, but that was about it. The scotch had hit him hard, and let's just say his tot didn't want to become a tater. I'll let you all figure that one out. And that was that. However, the next morning Kansas pulled a typical Kansas by apologizing for his behavior, because he didn't mean it. Oh, silly boy, didn't you know at that point I was just using you right back? I had totally realized what a bag of shit you were, and come to find out a few weeks later, you had done the same thing to three other women in the club!

I'm glad I didn't continue to get sucked into that second go-around and waste any more time on him. The only thing I decided to start hittin' was another boxing bag. In another gym.

Absolutely No One

The 2014 holiday season was tough. It was the first time in forever that I didn't have a significant other, and my usual celebratory system was off, but I was doing a great job of faking it. Between the serial dating in between obsessing over Kansas and constant pondering of where my life was going, I hit a breaking point the first couple of days of 2015. Who wouldn't after that beautiful purge of feelings to Kansas right at the end? I felt as if I were trapped in an elevator, and I couldn't get out. So I did something very impulsive—I bought a ticket to Europe. For five weeks. Let's be real, I was running away. I would never have admitted it at the time, but yes, I was absolutely running away from my life. I was going to cross off some of those "fuck it" list items in the process. I figured I'd start in London, since I hadn't been there since I was about seven years old. I love London, and heading across the pond might be a good start. I hadn't spent a lot of time outside of London, and I was really looking forward to doing some new things, like going to the Royal Shakespeare Company (I go weak at the knees for William) and maybe seeing some castles, like Warwick or Sudeley. Nothing that would compare to the main event—Neuschwanstein Castle in Germany—but this would be a good pre-game. I had missed out on a trip to Germany that I was supposed to take with my ex-husband, and I was going to be making up for it, you better believe it.

Traveling alone has never been a problem for me. I don't get nervous eating alone in a restaurant or wandering unknown streets. I am content being by myself. It might be an only-child thing. I have a fair amount of friends who are only children, and we really do enjoy time and space to ourselves. I also give kudos to my parents for taking me abroad at such an early age, when experiencing different cultures allowed me to have respect for others in their environment. I like to learn about and try new things. I figured this trip would give me the opportunity to reflect on the divorce. I think people assume because you file for a divorce, that's your grieving process. Instead, the process continues for a very long time. Sometimes years. At this point it had only been a few months since I was jumping in that pool in my wedding dress, which was definitely not a sign of someone handling their emotions well. I hoped this trip would also allow me to believe in myself again and gain independence by moving forward with a new approach to the next chapter of my life. I think in general, I just needed to grieve alone, so why not do it away from home, exploring places I may never have a chance to see again?

I arrived in London to bitter-cold weather. I don't know why I picked winter to do this self-exploration trip, but I figured it went with my mood. One of the best things about traveling in winter is that there are not many crowds at the tourist attractions. When you're on a trip, it's so easy to have a plan, but things change, just as life does. I played destination roulette for most of my trip. For those of you that don't know what that is, you put a list of cities on pieces of paper in a hat, a cup, whatever, then choose them at random. Whichever one comes up, that's where you go. I met some of the friendliest people, ate some of the best food, and saw some things people only dream of seeing. I felt so thankful to be in such incredible places.

Germany was one of the highlights of the trip, since the Neuschwanstein Castle had been calling me for years and was anticipating my arrival, of course. So you can imagine how bummed I was that I had been sick with a cold for nearly two weeks of the trip. It wasn't going to stop me from doing all the things I had planned on doing though. Because of my cold, all the walking and the trains were starting to wear me down, so I caved and rented a car. This all sounded logical, until I was thirty seconds out of the rental-car parking lot and realized that (a) I didn't know how to speak German and (b) I didn't know how to drive in snow and ice. I had only driven in that situation once, right out of college on a film set, and said I would never do that again. Still, since I had rented an Audi and had one at home, I felt very confident in the car's ability to take me where I needed to be. The slogan should be "Audi: there is no other." Off I went onto the autobahn, where all people should learn to drive. I was in the fast lane, as I tend to drive fast, but apparently not fast enough. I didn't know that the average speed on the autobahn was there is none. It's "get the fuck out of the way" speed. I arrived in the town of Füssen, which is at the bottom of Neuschwanstein Castle, and was too excited to sleep. I was also coughing up a lung, but nothing a good hot toddy couldn't fix. Waking up the next morning felt like the morning of my high-school track meets. Today was the day. It had snowed the night before and was cloudy but crisp. It was beautiful. I drove over to the castle base, parked, and went to purchase my ticket. *What?* There were only two options for that day. Due to weather, I could walk up the hill (which was a mile) or ride in the buggy thing (which would take a long time—no gas), and I'd have to wait in line. Apparently because of the bad weather from the last couple of days, the buses could not go up the main street to the castle. Well, this just wasn't going to work for me. I came all this way. I almost went into internal Lauren tantrum mode, when I stopped. I said to myself, *What do I have to do? Where do I have to be? I'm dressed in* ski clothes. *Yes, I have a cold. Yes, it may get worse. But this is a once-in-a-lifetime opportunity.* I decided to walk up the hill. Not many people were walking. I think there were only about four of us who chose that option. We didn't really walk together, as we were all at different paces, but it was the most incredible walk I have experienced in my life to date. Seeing the snow on the trees and mountains. Seeing the snow on the castle. Watching the castle get closer and closer. It was so serene. When I got to the top, I cried. Not like a big boo-hoo, but just a few tears of the beauty of finally being somewhere I wanted to be. I enjoyed every inch of that castle. I even went to the secret bridge that they close during winter because it's too dangerous. Totally worth the picture. Although I was enjoying this part alone, I so badly wished I had someone to share it with. Travel is such a big part of my life, and these moments are important to me. After I returned to the hotel, I wondered, *What makes someone happy without another human being?*

The last leg of my trip was spent in Barcelona. Picasso never fails me, just like Mr. Shakespeare. I hadn't been to Barcelona in ten years, so I felt it was time for a reunion. The last time I was there was right when I met the "big mistake," and I figured this was a good way to start my single life over again. Ironically, I happened to arrive on Valentine's Day. It's a great day for all the #partyofone people like me that just want to be reminded of true love everywhere—gag! I figured why not splurge on a club room–level deal on the last few days of this amazing journey. Of course, I still didn't know what lesson I had learned or how much reflection I had *really* done yet, but it didn't matter, because I was in Barcelona! The concierge gal, Luna, was very helpful about the city and even gave me her personal number if I needed anything. She was bummed because her trip to the States had been canceled (Atlanta, ironically), and she would be around the next few days if I needed anything. I set off for the evening to my tapas restaurant of choice. I gave them my name, but there was no need—I was the only person that booked a table for one in the *entire* restaurant. Oh joy. They escorted me upstairs to a table, which happened to be in the middle of the restaurant, like I was on display, and checked on me every few minutes. They felt bad that I was there alone and, *gasp*, single. I got to thinking, *Can I live without a man and be content on my own?* I knew I could, I just needed to figure out how. That was the hard part. I had started off the evening so excited for the adventure, but all this thinking was making me sad. Here these nice waiters were, just trying to make me feel good about not being alone, but actually being alone and thinking about being alone was making me feel more alone. We get so wrapped up in focusing on how someone else makes us feel (example: *una sola* at a restaurant) that we forget to make ourselves happy. This trip was essentially to make myself happy, and damn it, I had two nights left. I was going to end on a high note. I texted Luna.

Luna invited me over to her flat that evening, which is a very *big* deal in the Spanish culture. She greeted me downstairs, and we proceeded to walk up eighty-four steps (*I'm never going to get over this cold,* I thought). We decided to go out with some of her friends. My last night in Barcelona was a night I'll never forget. Here I was, sitting in one of the most beautiful cities, with a local, experiencing a culture that was unique. I had a date with not only a new friend but also the city. I felt like I had a backstage pass. After the bars closed, we walked around for hours to see some of the historic buildings lit up in all their glory. I could tell Luna was going to become a lifelong friend. Sometimes you just know about some people. Their demeanor. Their graciousness. We had a long hug at the Arc de Triomf at five a.m., then I begrudgingly headed back to my hotel to pack and take a cab to the airport.

Those five weeks changed my life. I realized that I was going to be OK. Luna gave me hope. Being a single, independent woman about my age living in a foreign country, working, and living her best life as we Americans say, she gave me hope that I could not only have that but also go back to doing what I loved to do career-wise. There were a lot of things I needed to think about. Life had so many new experiences to offer. Maybe not all would be as grand as a trip to Europe, but I knew I had so many things yet to discover back home. I didn't want to stop traveling though. The goggles had come off, and I saw the world differently. I was ready for the challenges ahead, and I was going to take dating, love, and heartbreak by the balls.

Gator

Not long after I had gotten back from Europe, I decided it was time for a fresh start. The tail end of the trip really had me soul-searching for some new changes, and even though I didn't know exactly where or what I wanted from life, I knew living in the house that I had shared with Jesse Pinkman wasn't it. Even though his stuff wasn't there anymore, I still just saw evidence of him everywhere. Also, the south Florida town, though it had my parents and a few close friends, didn't have the career opportunities I was looking for if I was going to dive back into entertainment. But at this point, I was just looking for a place to start over, and the first step I could think of was to move back to where happiness all began: Atlanta, Georgia.

I always had a good support system in Atlanta. I still had friends there from childhood that I kept in touch with and some I even saw a few times a year, like my friend Sarah Anne, whom I had known since birth. My biological sisters lived not too far outside the city, so it'd be nice to see them more often, and the idea of living in a metropolitan city seemed exciting. This was going to be the real world. I wasn't going to be with a husband or parents. I was going to be by myself. In a big city. In a high-rise apartment. I was going to be like Carrie Bradshaw, but on a minor scale. Which I was totally fine with. Leaving the house was bitter-sweet, but I think I had exhausted myself so much over my marriage and divorce that I looked at it more as good riddance. That house could be someone else's problem now. I cried a lot during the divorce, but the day I left the house, no tears fell. I had started to heal. Atlanta that fall was my fresh start, but first a pit stop for Halloween shenanigans with some college friends was overdue.

That Halloween weekend I had decided to visit some friends in St. Augustine, Florida, my other old stomping grounds, where I graduated from a local college with a bachelor's degree in the wonderful study of communications. (You know, the degree you get when you want to crush the job market as soon as you graduate.) Halloween is a big deal in that town. If you don't know, St. Augustine is the oldest city in the United States, and a big part of it is haunted. Whether you believe in ghosts or not, some strange things have happened to me, as well as some of my friends here. But if I actually took the time to tell you, it would take up this whole book. Just go visit and see for yourself. It's worth it. Trust me. Anyway, I was really looking forward to spending another Halloween there reliving the good old days. The night before, I got a text from a friend of a friend named Gator. We had known each other on a very casual level for a couple of years at that point, mostly attending the same parties. He was looking forward to all of us hanging out, and since we both were coming off breakups, he offered to help me out in the other department if I was up for it.

> Gator: Hey, sorry to hear about everything.

> Me: Thanks. I appreciate it.

> Gator: Looks like we're both in the same boat and could use some fun this weekend.

> Me: Totally agree.

> Gator: I'm down for some other type of fun this weekend too.

> Me: . . . I don't do drugs.

Gator: LOL, no! I don't mean that!

At first, I had no idea what he was talking about. *I don't do drugs?* What the hell kind of line is that, Lauren? Still being clueless on the dating game, I basically had to force him to spell out the proposition of having sex with him. No one had ever really proposed this to me before. Sex? Just two people having planned sex? Usually how this went down in college was at a party already wasted. We didn't really talk about getting together, as it was already happening. There was no talky-talky, just doey-doey. I wasn't sure how to react. I went with the "let's see how things go tomorrow" answer, because I didn't want to put any pressure on the situation. I also had, well, no idea how to respond; I was internally freaking out. A part of my brain had forgotten all about the good ol' years with Cool and the gang, and somehow I felt like a virgin all over again. *What if I do it wrong? Does my pussy even still work? I haven't had to shave down there in forever.*

Casual sex. How different is it at twenty-eight than at twenty? At twenty-eight, one is more selective about locations, grooming, and definitely morning breath. When you sleep with someone in college, it can happen anywhere: dorm rooms, cars, closets in the middle of house parties (yes, that did happen once at Senior House). The sky was the limit. Who cares, because it was just sex, right? I could count on one hand how many times I had had sex since my ex-husband and I had split up. Zero. Zero times. Winter bush had stayed all year long, even through summer and well into fall.

I decided that if things naturally went in a direction where Gator and I found ourselves alone to do the deed, then I would take the plunge into this casual sex world, although it had changed . . . and apparently so had I. (I mean, since when did I start calling it *the deed* anyway?)

This year I had decided to go antislut for my costume, which was a change for me. Every year since I could remember, I always opted toward slutty on Halloween. Even in high school, with my strict parents, I would leave the house as Belle and change at a friend's house into a Playboy bunny. In college, my costumes consisted of something I bought from Hustler. But this year I was going to do it differently. I had always wanted to go decked out as the Wicked Witch of the West, and since I had the nice "fuck it" list, this was one of the things I wanted to do with my new freedom. I was in no mood to care about anyone or anything at the time. This would be the perfect opportunity to check another thing off my list. This is what I wanted to do, and I was going to do it—full-blown green makeup and all.

Gator lived in downtown St. Augustine, about half a mile or so from the bars. When we all arrived at his house, I felt so . . . awkward. And not because of my award-winning costume—I mean, I rocked that shit. We were like two high schoolers who knew they were

going to lose their virginity on prom night. It's like
our friends were the chaperones, and we had a huge
secret. However, I still wasn't sold on the idea. What
if I wasn't ready to re-lose my virginity? I hadn't slept
with another man in so long. What if . . . OMG . . .
what if I cried? Do people cry during sex? What if I
farted? This was starting to seem like a really bad idea.
But then again, I was horny as hell. I thought about
having sex a lot, and I knew I did need to get laid. So
many friends had encouraged me to get on Tinder,
which had become popular right around the time of
my divorce, but I didn't even know how to really use it.
It was all so overwhelming.

I love St. Augustine during the holidays. Starting
at Halloween and lasting through New Year's, there
are many fun events downtown. The lights, the colors,
the music—it really is one of the best cities for getting
yourself into the holiday spirit. And at Halloween, the
costume contests are the best. Each bar has a theme
and different prizes. The drinks do runneth over, however. We eventually scampered downtown for eyeball
shots. (Not to be confused with taking straight vodka
in the eyes like teenagers do to get drunk.) There's an
episode of *How I Met Your Mother* that talks about
how nothing good happens after two a.m. Well, I had
pushed my time up. Nothing good happens after midnight. Even though I was still a couple of years from the
big three-zero, when out with friends, I would notice I
would get tired quicker than others. I think I had been

so used to being in a married routine and not having late nights out that I was ready to be in my fat pants watching a *Breaking Bad* marathon by ten p.m.

Around eleven p.m., I was over getting pushed and shoved at the crowded bar. I knew my friends wouldn't want to leave, and I didn't want to be the party pooper. Last call wasn't for another three hours; that would've ended friendships right there if I had asked them to take me home, so I told them I was tired and leaving.

Gator noticed I was heading out and offered to walk me back to his place, where the car was parked. *Of course he did.* Such chivalry. When we reached his house, he invited me inside. And here we go . . . you know, the "dance around the subject" kind of talk. "So, what did you think of those eyeball shots?" he said. "They were really gross," I replied. I mean, it was so painstakingly uncomfortable, like two kids in middle school waiting on their first kiss. I was twelve years old all over again. Eventually he made a move to kiss me, but my hair got stuck in my green face paint. Classy. He said that if I wanted to shower off and change, I was welcome to.

I knew we were heading down to Fuck Town, so I made my way to the bathroom. (Because apparently nobody wants to fuck a green witch.) While I was in the shower, he poked his head in the bathroom asking if I needed anything. I didn't know what to say to that. "Sure, I'll take some dick if you're offering," might have worked, but instead I just said, "No, thanks." I looked down at my poon. It looked like a fourteen-year-old had cut the neighbor's lawn with scrapbooking scissors. Remember in elementary school when you had those scissors that would cut different shapes? Some had zigzags, some had swirls? Well, it looked like my poon hair, or lack thereof, was an art project gone wrong. I was just going to have to get over it. I had put my big-girl pants on before, and I'd have to do it again and think up an excuse for him to not put his head down there. "Sorry, out of order, spring cleaning." Him: "But I . . ." Me: "I said good day, sir!"

I toweled off and peeked my head out of the bathroom. Was it too late to back out? I saw his bedroom door open, and with the towel wrapped around me, tiptoed over. How had I become so conservative at my young age? This was the first time I felt like I was about to have legit adult sex. He had left one of his shirts for me to throw on (you know, like a gentleman). He came into the bedroom, and we talked for a bit (More talking? Seriously?). I couldn't even tell you what about at this point. You know the sound the adults make when they're talking in the *Peanuts* cartoons? *Whah, whah, whah, whah . . .* I was afraid if we kept going in this direction, I'd either (a) fall asleep on him or (b) my poon tingle would fizzle out, and I'd lose interest. I already scrounged up the nerve to have planned casual sex. Mama ready to go, man. Stop acting like a woman!

Of course, when it started it was bumpy, literally and figuratively. I hadn't had sex in so long that I was hilariously out of practice when it came to dirty talk. For example, while we were doing it doggie, and I was holding on to the handrails of the headboard, I blurted out, "This is nice. Is this Pottery Barn?" That's when you know you're a homeowner. I'm a lady in the streets but a conscientious shopper in the sheets. I also didn't know how adventurous I should be or not be. I mean, how were the kids having sex these days?

So, how was this adult sex I was so anxious about? Fine. It wasn't great, it wasn't bad. For my first fuck postdivorce, I was honestly just glad it was over. When we were finished, he laid in bed and popped open a La Croix and a bag of Doritos. Which he didn't even offer to share. La Croix is my drink of choice, to those that know me or ever see my Instagram, which is close enough to knowing anyone in this day and age. And Doritos? Cool Ranch all the way! Whenever I invite guests over, I always share my snacks. I was immediately reminded of this bit from one of my favorite comedians, Theo Von. "What about some chips? Nothing washes down a fuck like some chips. Wanna split a bag of chips wit' daddy?" Every time I hear Theo's bit on that it takes me back to that night with Gator. The man who didn't even offer to split that fucking bag of chips with me after we did it in five different positions! And I was hungry! Anyway, it was late. I figured I'd just sleep here, even though that wasn't really what I wanted to do. I like my space when I sleep. I don't need to be hugged or spooned throughout the night. I am perfectly content with my own pillow and my side of the bed, and this bed, come to find out, was not Pottery Barn material.

Gator, on the other hand, liked to spoon. As I lay trapped underneath his arm, afraid to breathe, I wondered what Carrie Bradshaw would do. Do I shift and see if he will move over? Do I do the Chandler Bing tuck and roll? I suddenly realized I get most of my life advice from sitcoms. (I'm sure I'll break out some Jack McFarland eventually.)

I tried the shift first. Didn't work. I was wide awake and laughing at myself as usual. I could reach my phone, miraculously, as I don't have long arms. I texted my friend, asking if she wanted me to pick her up from the bar and take her home, because it clearly wasn't working out with Cool Ranch breath. The response was affirmative, so I had the perfect out.

Slowly, I slid off the bed, threw on Gator's large T-shirt and my underwear, grabbed my friend's car keys, and walked out. We were coming back over tomorrow to get the rest of our stuff, so I didn't think I needed pants (and the shirt was kinda like a short dress anyway). I was just driving across the bridge. No biggie. I walked out, got in the Toyota RAV4, and started to back out of his unpaved driveway. After moving a couple of feet, the car would not back up any farther. I got out, checked the tires—they were fine. *That's weird,* I thought. Back in the car. Reverse. No go. What the hell was happening?

I climbed back out and tried to shift some dirt around the car. Tried again. Nothing. The car was completely stuck. At this point, it was one thirty in the morning. I had no pants, no shoes, no purse. Crap. I was going to have to slink back in and hope I wouldn't disturb Gator.

Now, the thing about St. Augustine is that the houses are old. Colonial style. Sometimes, when you exit a door, the only way you can reenter is with a key. Even if you didn't lock the door. Being that it was after midnight, post a couple of drinks, post a stressful fuck, I had forgotten this. So when I went up to the door to let myself in, lo and behold it was locked. I knocked. No answer. I called. No answer. Was Gator in a fucking coma? I phoned an out-of-state friend. I don't know why I thought she could help. I was in survival mode. She just laughed and enjoyed my moment of extreme panic. No help there. A car drove by, and I flagged it down. It was a teenage boy who was delivering late-night pizzas. He, of course, was probably getting a boner from my new "Halloween costume." So much for not going slutty this year! Unfortunately, he was of no help, but he did offer me a slice of pizza.

I kept calling my friends on rapid fire. No one was answering. The only thing I could do at this point was walk into town and look for them. I searched the car for shoes. My friend wears a size five. Although I wear a six and a half wide, I managed to squeeze my fat feet into her boots and started hoofing it to town.

Cue the red and blue lights. Out of all nights to get pulled over by a cop, this would be the night. Good thing my new costume was townie hooker. I tried to explain my story to the officer. He laughed—a lot. I assured him this was all true, to no avail. But since I gave him a hearty laugh, and since he felt bad for me, he gave me a ride to the bar. (Thanks, Officer Mendez!) I found my friends in the second bar I looked—Tradewinds never seems to fail. It's almost like they hadn't even noticed I left. There was no point in bitching at them for not answering their phones in my time of need, so I figured the only thing at that point was to get drunk and down a couple of shots at last call. So, I did. Hell, I wasn't the worst dressed in the bar that night anyway.

The next morning in the cab over to Gator's (Uber wasn't around in St. Augustine yet), my friend's boyfriend said to me, "Did you check the parking brake?" Now, why would I check the parking brake in Florida? For the big ass mountain it's parked on? Never in all the years I lived in Florida did I ever use a parking brake. Apparently, Toyotas have great parking-brake safety, because that was the only reason the car didn't move.

I never imagined having a re–walk of shame, but I guess there's a first for everything. After telling Gator all that he missed while he was out cold, and having a good laugh, there was no awkward "Yeah, I'll call you" or "That was fun. We should do it again sometime." It was strictly sex, no strings attached. I haven't spoken with him since that night, but I am thankful that he taught me a valuable lesson. I realized that yes, you can have unemotional, unattached adult sex. It's possible. It may be disappointing, or it may be the best sex of your life. It may result in a hell of an odd adventure. It may not come with Doritos, but it is possible. In the meantime, I continued to be on the lookout for new bed frames in my new high-rise apartment . . . in my new city of Atlanta.

The Breakup

I hate breakups. I don't know one person who feels differently, unless you're a narcissist and get off on them. Even if you know you aren't right for each other and it's a mutual thing, breakups still suck. I wish this next chapter were about two lovers who realized they were just better off as friends, but it's not. While living in Atlanta, I had one of the most confusing, sad, unexplainable breakups, and it wasn't even with a boyfriend.

As you read earlier in the story, Sarah Anne and I were two peas in a pod. Our parents were very close at the time, and they had each become our godparents. We were both only children and became immediate best friends. We were Anne Shirley and Diana Barry, we were Rachel and Monica, we were Carrie Bradshaw and Samantha Jones (although it's unfortunate they're not friends in real life). We were together at every holiday, birthday, weekend tea party—we were best friends, whether we chose to be or not. I use that phrase deliberately. We didn't choose to be best friends. Our parents chose that for us.

I admit, Sarah Anne was the better sharer in the beginning. I remember seeing a video of us when we were probably only two or so. I was playing with an elephant, and she wanted to play with it too. She kept reaching for it, and I kept snatching it back. In my eyes, there were other toys she could play with . . . go get your own. (Sigh, such a "fend for yourself" kind of mentality at the ripe old age of two.) Our moms had similar teaching styles in manners, etiquette, and discipline (which I'm so thankful for), but they had . . . different styles. Sarah Anne was always dressed in Laura Ashley, which always reminded me of a tablecloth. But then again, my mom's fashion choices for me consisted of big bows, puffy dresses, and white stockings that made my legs and crotch itch so bad. But it was the late eighties and early nineties. Those were the trends. Sarah Anne was homeschooled, while I was basking in Ring Pop delight at the Christian school. I would say I probably matured a little faster than her, but in the grand scheme of things, this probably isn't saying much considering the stories in this book. By mature, I mean I was getting into boys and she was into, well, dinosaurs and *Jurassic Park*. And by dinosaurs, I mean she could've been Ross Geller's niece: she knew all the names, had dinosaur pajamas—it was all she talked about. I was already on my third boyfriend in fifth grade (sorry, Tommy), and she was planning her future as a paleontologist. We just were very different. I liked sports. She played the flute. She read. I did only if it was for school. I just felt like I couldn't connect with someone who was supposed to be my best friend.

When we moved to Florida in 1999, she and her mom rode down with us the long ten hours to settle us in, while Dad finished up some business in Atlanta. I don't really remember much of what we did besides unpack and hang by the water, but we eventually said our goodbyes and promised to keep in touch via phone (she wasn't allowed to have an AIM account yet). Off they went. I didn't cry, and I don't think she did either. We weren't that emotional about our friendship. I can't recall the next time I saw her, to be honest, but it had to have been some holiday when her family came down to visit at Thanksgiving or Christmas. We went up to Atlanta a lot too. So I know we saw each other a couple of times a year. And when I got more involved in sports and she ended up going to a private Christian school, our lives became too busy to really keep in touch.

During our junior year of high school, she invited me to her homecoming game, as I was going to be in town. When I got there I saw that she was this new person. She had friends, *guy* friends. She had grown boobs. She liked rap music. Who was this person? And what happened to the dinosaurs? I mean, I get that people change, but where had that person been hiding all along? I almost didn't know what to think. This Sarah Anne was fun. Right after she graduated high school and after my first year of college, we went off to Europe with my parents. (Keep up, people! You heard about this!) We drank our asses off and were on top of the world. I think she had her first make-out session with this French guy in the most amazing club known to man at the time (in our eyes, at least) in Monaco, Jimmy'z. Those were the days.

Our fun continued through college until my relationship with Jesse Pinkman started becoming more serious. She seemed to struggle to understand what it was like to be committed to someone, as she had never had a boyfriend. We still partied and went to concerts, and when it came time for me to plan my wedding, of course I asked her to be my maid of honor. Who else was I going to ask? She had been my best friend my whole life.

For some reason, on the day of the wedding I wasn't really in the mood to have all the girls get ready with me. I felt like it'd be too much drama—there was too much drinking the night before, and a lot I don't even remember. In addition, there was some stuff that had gone on the last couple of years between Sarah Anne and me that had put us on different pages. A lot of this I feel was because of my relationship with Jesse Pinkman. It was a tough spot for me to be in. We had become different people, but we didn't know how to

handle being different people, because we were supposed to be best friends. I had married a verbally abu-
sive, manipulative jerk that I was blinded by and only
saw what I thought were charming qualities, and she
saw right through him, along with everyone else. But
unfortunately at that young age, we hadn't set boundaries in our friendship. It isn't all on her, in her defense.
She probably hated seeing her friend marry the wrong
guy. After my marriage, we did continue to visit each
other, but it seemed there was always tension when my
husband was around, which made me feel less con-
nected to her. She was single and wanted to go to fun
bars in Atlanta, and I was spiraling into a depression
and probably wasn't a fun friend at that time anyway.
She liked indie music and wanted to enjoy the scene,
and, well, I just wanted to enjoy a quiet night away
from the chaos that was my marriage. And when 2013
hit and the complications in my marriage and the
legalities of his situations started, my relationships
with friends fell to the wayside. I had other things to
tend to. I was in a dark hole for about a year and a half.
But the move back to Atlanta seemed to kick off our
friendship again.

To me, Atlanta will always be home, and it was
great to be back. Atlanta wasn't just a fresh start for
me—it kind of felt like a fresh start for our friendship. I
am reminded of the song "Goodbye Earl" by the Dixie
Chicks. Wanda and Mary Ann. Can we guess who's
who in that story? It seemed like we put Earl to bed and

were ready to move on from any tension we had in the past. We would go out to all the great restaurants and go on walks through the BeltLine and treat ourselves to margs and guac, not to mention wingy and fat-pants night. Side note: This is how wingy and fat-pants night got started. Every time I would come into town before moving back to Atlanta, we would wind up one night feeling lazy and ordering in wings and having wine and staying in our sweatpants. It's a tradition now. I don't know how many others she wing-cheats on me with, but it doesn't matter. It's still fun. (Fox Bros in Atlanta all the way—you can keep that JR Crickets gar-bage. People like it only because they heard about it on the TV show *Atlanta*. It's gone downhill. Fox Bros is steady as a rock. I digress.) We used to do spontaneous things, like one Saturday when we decided to get a kid-die pool, fill it with water, put it in the front yard by the street, make some margs, and turn up the music. Even the dog was enjoying herself, running around and col-lecting pine cones for toys. We were straight out of a Jeff Foxworthy stand-up special. It was glorious. Both being only children, we had a lot of experience figuring out ways to be easily entertained. (Like the one time we wore snorkel gear to see a movie.)

Sarah Anne was there for me when I was trying to figure out my next steps after the divorce. I was there for her when she was contemplating quitting her job and moving to New York. She helped me move into my apartment in midtown and even organized my closet. There is nothing I loathe more than organizing a closet. I hate hanging up clothes. I hate folding clothes. But she did it. I would pick her up from the airport late at night. We spent so much time together the first six months I moved to Atlanta, it was almost like we were dating. It felt so good to have my friend around, but was it healthy?

We had a few incidents where I felt boundaries were pushed though. At times into the next year, I felt she was being a little selfish and not considerate of my feelings. Sometimes I didn't want to say yes to everything, and I didn't want to go out all the time, or I didn't want to go to a concert, or whatever the thing may be, and she didn't understand. It had been only a little over a year since my divorce, and I was starting to learn it was OK to say no. I was also learning to make my own decisions without anyone else. That must have been hard for her, because we had spent so much time together, and I think I was still learning to set boundaries. I have to admit, my approach to things wasn't very good at the time. I definitely hadn't learned the best way on that yet. I know I was selfish. It is OK to be selfish sometimes, but communication and the approach are so important, and I think that may be where I fell flat.

I had enrolled in a playwriting class at a local college to get some creative juices flowing and decided to head back to England for spring break with my dad. Sarah Anne and I had been spending a lot of time together the last few weeks, and, in all honesty, I needed a bit of a break. We all get like that. I received a text from her at the airport, suggesting we get matching tattoos. That idea didn't interest me, and I think I responded that she could get one if she wanted to. But Sarah Anne didn't seem to like how that came across. And right there, our friendship stopped existing. From my perspective, it seemed she didn't understand that I didn't have to do what she wanted me to do. I am my own person, and she is her own person, and we are not the same. I think two things were happening for me at that moment in time leading to this breaking point: (1) I was tired of someone not respecting my boundaries. Not understanding I didn't always want to go out. I didn't always want someone poking their fork into my food or saying, "Can I have a fry?" and not even waiting for me to respond before just taking it off my plate. Tired of someone saying they'll be there in five minutes and arriving twenty minutes later. Just tired of the disrespect. It reminded me of my ex-husband. I felt suffocated. I was triggered. And (2) I was jealous. She seemed to have it all in her career, she was pretty, she was popular, and she was all the things I used to be when we were in high school and the beginning of college, but I chose marriage at an early age, and things derailed somewhat. And now I was trying to do the things she was already doing. I was looking for the career. I was living in the big city. I was attempting to do this dating thing. I didn't want to mark myself with a tattoo, which almost made me feel like it symbolized a commitment to someone else. I wanted to be free. I had just gotten out of an eight-year commitment with someone that didn't end so well. We were supposed to be friends that supported each other to find someone *else* to be committed to, not each other. So I think it was all those things that had been festering inside of me, and I had just had enough.

A week of not talking while I was in England turned into a month, then into six months, and all of a sudden it was Christmas. There were times I wanted to text her something funny that happened that only she would appreciate, or I was having wings and thought of her, or if I had had a horrible date and needed to vent to someone. Every year on our birthdays and Christmas, we always sent each another gifts, so that year I did email a gift card to keep the tradition alive. Our parents were still friends, and I wasn't going to ruin their friendship just because ours no longer existed. My father told me that people go in phases in your life and that maybe we just needed time apart.

Right after Christmas, I decided to be the better person and write her an email. In it, I explained my feelings in detail. It wasn't to hate on her or to hate on me or the friendship, but to clear the air. A week later she responded with her own thoughts in a mature manner. A couple of months went by, and we took it slow, being respectful of each other's feelings. I wish I could say that she's this changed person since that email hash out and that she's a mature, boundary-obeying, selfless individual all the time, but she's not. I do see some of the same patterns, and I've taken it for what it is. Our friendship has been different. There are things I still appreciate about her. I no longer mind that she picks food off my plate; I try to get enough for both of us. I know that I can count on her when I'm craving Mexican food, and we can walk the BeltLine and find a good margarita, and she will eat all the chips and hog the salsa. Just because we are different or she doesn't make the choices I wish she would make sometimes doesn't mean I don't love her or want what's best for her. I'm not a perfect person either. I do know that I try and learn from my mistakes and not repeat them. I learn from my breakups, whatever kind they are— business, boyfriends, dog sitter, you name it. I didn't realize how much this friend, who wasn't chosen by me to be my friend, meant to my life until we didn't speak for ten months. Those tests in life hurt, and they suck, but sometimes we need them. Sometimes they truly aren't mendable. Sometimes they may not be ready to fix for years. But sometimes we need to look at all the facts and ourselves and what we've done and accept the situation for what it is. You never know what someone else is going through—a breakup or a job loss or personal family issues that they don't talk about but they project onto the friendship. Back in 2010, Sarah Anne said this in her speech at my wedding. She was referring to my husband and me at the time, but I think this applies to our friendship now. As Carrie Bradshaw said on an episode of *Sex and the City*, "If you find someone who loves the you *you* love, well then that's just fabulous."

Rita Right Eye and The Rolling Backpack

When I was a kid, my babysitter called me Rita Right Eye. Ever since I could see the light of day, I wore glasses. No joke, I wore them from the time I was eighteen months old until I was about thirteen because of a lazy eye. And for a few years in elementary school, I wore an eye patch. While it made for a fun time at Halloween parties, the other 364 days out of the year were a different story. In fourth grade, when we were figuring out if boys had cooties or not and other girls were in training to be the next Regina George (we all remember *Mean Girls*, right?), being the girl with the eye patch was just . . . not . . . cool. My mom tried to make it fun. She bought me glasses of all different colors. Green, blue, hot pink. I even had multicolored glasses. When it came time to get the dreaded patch, my mom got me a rainbow patch, a star patch, and even a unicorn patch. And while I appreciated her efforts, no patch would ever prevent the emotional damage or the amounts of money I would spend on therapy years later.

My babysitter was a guy—to some of you that may be weird, but he was a family friend. Anyway, he and I lived on the same street. He knew I was a theater geek and aspired to be an actress one day (look at me now). I would make him play diner or beauty parlor or some type of production after school. I guess there was some foreshadowing there.

So Babysitter called me Rita every time he came to dine at my basement playhouse diner. In Georgia, most houses have basements where many kids reenact the greatest sword fights ever fought or the best performances of "Over the Rainbow." I chose to be in a diner. (I seemed to like the simple things then. Oh, how things change.) But Rita didn't just stick to the basement—oh no, she came everywhere. I hated when Babysitter would shout out, "Rita Right Eye!" as I rolled my cool rolling backpack around the school grounds with my friends and their regular backpacks. (Only a few of us were cool enough to own the new invention of a rolling backpack.) "Hey, Rita, why don't you roll that backpack out to Hollywood!" Babysitter would shout. Rita Right Eye was not going to work in Hollywood.

I needed a better stage name than Rita. Rita was old and lame, and it definitely was *not* going to get me to stardom. (No offense, Rita Hayworth, you were superhot in your day.) Neither was the patch. I needed to remedy my situation. If my eyes weren't going to fix themselves, I would get LASIK. If that didn't work, I'd track down a fucking witch to fix me with black magic. Whatever it took. I had goals. I had a plan. Fortunately, eventually I stopped having to wear the patch. I transitioned from glasses and braces to just braces. It was a rough few years. I somehow managed to still get a boyfriend. #winningagain

Anyway, I left the nineties and all the emotional scarring behind . . . so I thought. It wasn't until a Tinder date in Atlanta that the memories of Rita would get thrown right back in my face.

The guy was twenty-two. Are you any bit surprised? I'm living the single dream! I was twenty-eight at the time. It was my phase, OK? He was a security guard. He was hot, OK? In shape too. Maybe not the smartest. But nice to look at.

My neighbors were having a BBQ one evening, and I invited him. I figured if everything went well, then we could just walk across the street to my apartment and get down and then he could go on his way. He accepted the invite, and I headed over next door. The doorbell rings, and my friend answers. I'm in the living room area, and I can see that he has arrived. He walks in with . . . a rolling backpack. I kid you not. Just like Rita Right Eye had all those years ago. Henceforth, we will call him Rolly. I greet him, and my friend motions for him to put his stuff by the door. More like park it by the door. Did this guy just bring a rolling backpack to a BBQ? I had so many thoughts running through my mind. Did he think he was staying the week? Was he assuming we were having sex? Did he assume he was staying over? Was he homeless? I mean, the list is just endless. My friend's husband walks over and whispers to us, "Shall I call down to the front desk and ask for a bellman?" I decided not to judge, and I found Rolly pleasant. He was sober, which didn't scare me. (Might scare some people, but not me. I've dated a couple of sober people, and honestly, the sex can be better when there's no whiskey dick involved.) As the night came to a close, I thought, *Fuck it* and figured I might as well take advantage of this erect dick situation (because you don't know when drunk dick might appear).

So Rolly rolls his rolling backpack across the street to my apartment, and we get it on. (Is it just me, or do I sound like a pornographic Dr. Seuss?) He was fine. Not as good as Cool, but maybe that's because I had emotional damage from seeing a rolling backpack.

Rolly woke up to his alarm at five thirty in the morning (FML). He asked if I had any cereal. I, who don't eat breakfast often, oddly happened to have some cornflakes and milk (in case there is randomly a hurricane in Georgia). He sat there at the kitchen table with me, eating cornflakes at five thirty in the morning (hot, right?). He then packed up his rolling backpack (that contained a change of clothes, toiletries, and other items I tried to sneak a peek at), said he'd call me, and rolled out of my house. I never saw him again. I don't know where Rolly rolled that thing to next, but I heard that he was a man about town. A few of my acquaintances said they matched with Rolly on Tinder. None of them, however, wound up going out with him or having the backpack experience (guess I'm special?).

Rolly's backpack got me thinking. It reminded me of Babysitter. It reminded me of the diner. It reminded me of silly little dreams I had in that diner. Were they silly? Even though I had been working in Atlanta and getting back into entertainment, there were some opportunities for bigger steps. During the time spent in Atlanta, I had accomplished a few things that had put me back on track in the production world. Although I wasn't an actress and had given up that dream in college, my current career behind the camera was accelerating. I liked being a producer. I didn't want it to stall out. Maybe it *was* time for Rita to roll her backpack to Hollywood. So, after a few weeks of kicking this idea around and a project brewing, I put a plan in place. I was headed out west. Rita Right Eye, sans eye patch. I guess Babysitter knew all along that I had my sights set on LA . . . and this time, I could see much clearer.

Billy The Kid

Ah, Vegas. Sin City. Entertainment capital of the world. Glitter Gulch . . . shall I go on? No? I've never actually "sinned" in Vegas. Or had to go along with the saying "What happens in Vegas, stays in Vegas," because in my eyes, what happens there gets told to *all my friends*. At that time, when I'd been traveling to Vegas, it had been for work or for nondrinking spa trips with my friends. (I've learned Vegas is pretty fun not shitfaced too!) I had been living in Los Angeles all of one year, and this particular trip in December of 2017 was for production work. I arrived in town and headed straight to work. I hadn't slept well in about two weeks and had completely exhausted myself (which, unfortunately, is a reoccurring theme for people in the entertainment industry), so I couldn't wait for my quick work stint to be over so I could enjoy the town for one evening before heading back to LA to enjoy the holiday season. But the universe, as always, had others plans.

On this particular evening after work, I planned to go over to Bellagio, maybe play a few rounds of blackjack (stay on sixteen, hit on fifteen), head back to Planet Hollywood where I was staying (somehow I always miss Britney when she's in town . . . *sigh*, my inner tween will have to wait), and go to bed before driving back to LA the next day. I got halfway through those plans just fine and then, well . . . who needs a calendar app? The rodeo was in town for the week, and I was missing Georgia very much. I had only been in LA for a year and was a little homesick. After noticing all the handsome cowboys wandering the streets, I needed a taste of home and decided to check out one of the country bars where they were all gathering. The cute bartender informed me that with every drink I bought I would receive a free ride on the mechanical bull. Of course, I had no intention of riding that thing. I embarrass myself daily, but this was definitely not the time nor the place. I figured I could give my turn to someone who was drunk enough or . . . cute enough, as I had already been eyeing the gentleman across the ring from me. For the remainder of this story, we will call him Billy the Kid.

Billy the Kid was just like everything you heard in every country song. Cue Toby Keith, Dixie Chicks, "Save a Horse (Ride a Cowboy)." Lady Gaga's "John

Wayne" playing on repeat. (Thanks, girl, for making the album *Joanne* and showing how you can be city-girl sexy with a twist of country.) Billy the Kid had on a blue plaid shirt that looked great with his tan skin, wispy hair, ten-gallon hat—I mean, the guy was practically an ad for Wrangler jeans. I laughed under my breath and said to myself, *You are so fucked* (a conversation I tend to have with myself on a regular basis) as I sipped my Coors Light in between each person getting up to ride the bull, the country music playing, and eyed the TV every now and again to look as if I were nonchalant about it all. I couldn't help but eye him, too, but let's face it—he probably had a girlfriend back home somewhere. Then Billy the Kid got up and walked over to the bull, and the thoughts in my head were as follows: *He's riding the bull. Am I salivating? This bar is attached to a casino. Casinos are normally freezing, but I'm breaking a sweat right now. Are my nipples showing through my blouse? Would that really be a bad thing if they were? Pull it together. OK, he's lasting a while . . . oh no . . . he fell off. All right, he's walking back . . . and he just got on the damn thing again! He really seems to be enjoying that bull.* As I stared down at my Coors Light, I thought, *Well, I do have this extra ticket for the bull. Maybe I should give it to him? No, Lauren, don't be stupid. Yes, Lauren, be stupid.* That conversation lasted another five minutes in my head until I finally decided that I might as well go over and give him my ticket. *If we end up talking, great, and if not, I've got barely half a beer left, and I can just leave and call it a night.*

So, I adjusted my blouse, stood up straight, and headed over to Billy the Kid. I was shaking even though I tried to look confident. I tapped him on the shoulder, handed him my ticket, and made some awkward comment about the bull. I probably referenced how they used to have a steel bull on display in my condo building in Atlanta and someone drew balls on it or something. Very true. Very unladylike. He introduced himself as he leaned in over the noise, his hair brushing over his eyes. *Swoon.* He told me he was in town to compete in a roping event with his family. *Roping,* I thought. *WTF is roping?* (Being the city girl that I am, I do not know much about all this rodeo stuff. I once went to some county fair back in college in North Carolina with some friends and met a guy who was aspiring to be a bull rider. He had explained some of this stuff to me later that evening (in his bedroom, of course), and it seemed fascinating. (But then again, anything seems fascinating when a hot guy is on top of you. That's as close as I've come to understanding this type of life. But, back to Vegas . . .) Billy the Kid admitted he was too shy to talk to me earlier, and we got to chatting. He had just gotten out of a ten-year relationship with his fiancée a few months back. (Hey, I know how that goes.) He was so polite, said yes ma'am, was remarkably attentive. He reminded me of home, of the South. This was his first trip to

Vegas, and they were staying at the campgrounds of the competition.

We stepped outside on the top level of the strip so he could grab a smoke. Not something I go for in a guy, but I was enjoying the evening. The weather was perfect. There was a really awful nineties cover band playing on the deck, and we started dancing. It felt like we were in high school, yet it was oddly romantic. Pause and think about that for a second. When is the last time *you* were dancing on the street, living in the moment? Doesn't happen every day, does it? And then, under Sin City lights, I said, "Are you going to kiss me or not?" And he did. We stood people watching a little while longer, then had another few drinks on the deck, listening to the band. He mentioned he was coming to LA from Northern California, where he lived on his farm, at the end of December with his mother. He said I was the "type of person he could introduce to his mama." Whoa. Isn't that something that you say down the road to someone? I tried hard to keep my cool as the conversation went on. It was getting late, and he was competing the next morning in a rodeo event. He said I should come. I thought that was a pretty bold invite, considering we had just met, but I was interested in seeing how this all would pan out. I didn't know if he was going to take a taxi home or what, but at this point I think we knew what we both wanted.

As we arrived at my room, the mood was calm. Neither of us was rushing. It felt peaceful. A part of me would love to get all *Fifty Shades of Grey* on you, but it wasn't like that. It was very romantic sex. There were some really hot parts, and if you could combine two songs of the moment, I'd say it was a combination of Bruno Mars's "Gorilla" and Chase Rice's "Ride." It was very, very good sex. Afterward, as much as I'm not a fan of cuddling, I was OK with it. I wanted to be next to him. We slowly drifted to sleep.

I rolled down my window and dust flew up into my black sports car. "Excuse me." *Cough.* Pause. "Excuse me," I said again to a man riding a horse. "Can you tell me where the entrance to Horseman's Park is?" I looked like I was straight from the city. Confused. Reminiscent of Reese Witherspoon in *Sweet Home Alabama*. Black shades. Black top. Thank God no heels though. I had apparently turned down the wrong road and into where the staging area was and was nicely redirected over to Billy the Kid. He greeted me with a kiss, of course. *Gawd, his lips.* He grabbed my hand and walked me over to his family. I still felt this whole situation was a bit bold, meeting someone's family so soon like that. Honestly, I don't know if I would invite someone to an important event in my life unless I really liked them. And if I was just going to fuck them and never see them again, I would have peaced-out imme- diately after sex. (*Ahem,* re–walk of shame.) Also, how awkward, knowing your son just slept with someone the night before. Anyway, they seemed like lovely people. I watched as they were warming up, getting everything ready for the competition, careful not to mention I was deathly afraid of horses. I did touch the horse a couple of times and repeated in my head *Please don't hurt me* over and over again as I plastered a fake smile on my face.

We sat together in between events, and every time we walked around, he would grab my hand and lead the way. A gentleman. Yes, I might have a bold, outgoing, assertive personality, but it is nice for a man to take the lead sometimes. At one point he opened up about a few things in his past and said something that, to this day, continues to stay with me: "Secrets don't make friends." We were supposed to hang out that evening after the event, but things didn't work out as planned, and his family left early to head back. I had planned to stay an extra night, just for him. I didn't really understand his excuse. He seemed really into me. His family seemed nice. I don't know if they were upset because he lost the event. I don't know if they secretly deemed it my fault. I was also upset with myself. I knew better than to change my plans for a man. Isn't that something we are taught by all our older and wiser family and friends? "Never change your life for a man." I was really disappointed.

I woke up the next day with so many thoughts running through my mind and a four-hour drive back to Los Angeles ahead of me. I'm not going to lie, I needed some John Newman, I needed some Lady Gaga, I needed some Taylor Swift and . . . I needed a little bit of a cry. I wasn't crying because I had slept with someone; I didn't feel used at all. That part was the least confusing bit out of the whole situation. I was crying because I had texted him after he had left, and although hurt, I was very understanding about him having to leave unexpectedly, though I wasn't really sure why. Once again, I think it had something to do with him losing the event. I mentioned that I would be interested in seeing him again sometime and didn't get a response. I was confused *because I met part of his family.* And mostly I was confused because of some of the things he said contradicted his actions. I think what men don't realize is that they don't have to say, "I want to see you again," and "I'll have to tell my friends about you," and blah blah blah. We don't need to hear it. We'd rather not hear it if it isn't true. That would save us so much hassle and hurt. I tried to look at things from his point of view though. He did just get out of a ten-year relationship. I thought back to when I got out of my marriage. Although I had wanted to be with someone, had wanted to feel needed, perhaps my heart wasn't completely ready at that time. So maybe his wasn't either, and I can't get upset at someone for that. Maybe he wasn't ready to let go of his past. Or maybe he went back home and realized he wanted to get back with her.

Billy the Kid finally texted me a couple of days later. We talked, and he apologized for being MIA. He mentioned there was some family stuff going on, but he wanted to see me again. We discussed potential dates to make that happen. New Year's Eve came up. He had some time off for the holidays, and although I was going away for Christmas, I would be back in California and could meet him somewhere for NYE weekend. I had a ticket to a John Mayer and Dave Chappelle show that I had bought back in July. John Mayer is my *favorite* musician ever, and I was really looking forward to seeing him on NYE. But I also knew that if there was a possibility of something coming to fruition with Billy the Kid, Mr. Mayer would just have to be placed on the back burner. I would wait a week, then sell the ticket. Billy the Kid and I started to make plans. He booked us a couple of nights at a winery, and I booked a couple of nights in Tahoe. This was going to be a very romantic long weekend. I was cautiously optimistic. I didn't know what to think, but the fact that he actually made a reservation and was excited about it made me go ahead and plan accordingly. We exchanged texts daily, and he'd send me cute things from work that reminded him of me, like the song "Like a Cowboy" by Randy Houser. Maybe my new year would be looking up.

I was headed to meet my parents in Park City, Utah, for Christmas. Ever since I was a kid, Park City has been a special place to me, even before I attended the Sundance Film Festival. It's where I learned how to ski and developed my love for Deer Valley chili. As I was sitting in the Delta lounge waiting to board my flight to Salt Lake City on December 23, I received a text from Billy the Kid.

> Hey, I'm really sorry, but I just don't think I can do New Year's. I'm just not in the right headspace and have a lot going on right now.

Although I wasn't surprised, my heart sank. I knew it was too good to be true.

The whole situation sucked. It made me go back to all my theories I had mulled over on the drive home from Vegas. The ex-fiancée. Not being ready. Needing time. I wish I had a real explanation. The fact that he still had the balls to text me through Christmas and look at all my Instagram stories and like my photos on Facebook didn't make me feel any better. Maybe he really was a jerk, but I doubt it. I know I did nothing wrong. I was so angry that I liked a guy. There were others I was sleeping with or going on dates with back in LA, but I didn't end up liking them like I liked this one. This one stung. This one pissed me off. Sometimes it works, sometimes it doesn't. I know that. But why wasn't it working for me? It had been over three years since the divorce, and I couldn't find a decent guy in LA, in Vegas, in Florida—I couldn't even find someone to date for more than three dates. I felt like my divorce had cursed me.

I was glad I didn't sell my ticket to John Mayer. I rang in the new year alone at the concert and met a wonderful girl at the VIP party who also was alone (super secure like that) and sitting two seats down from me.

I found out seven months later that Billy the Kid and his fiancée did get back together. I genuinely hope they are happy together. Even though I experienced hurt and loss out of that situation, it was some of the best sex, some of the most exciting feelings, and one of the most memorable trips to Vegas I've ever had. And hey, I did get his roping glove out of it as a souvenir. And always remember: you never know when your last kiss with someone will be, so make it a good one.

The Brit

"I dare you to run into the water shouting, 'Oh God, get out of the way!' and sink down as if you have major diarrhea," one of my sisters challenged me as we sat on a picturesque beach in the Caribbean in January of 2018. Considering we were in our thirties, I think we were making up for lost time, having never really grown up together. So, here we all sat, like Jeff Foxworthy's "Clampetts Go to Maui." But instead, it was "Jacksons Go to Jamaica." I like to refer to us as the Jackson 6. This particular January, I really needed my family. I needed my sisters. After an up-and-down year in the dating world and feeling so blue at the holidays after Billy the Kid, I really needed a great start to the new year. I tried not to work the entire trip, but things were picking up so quickly, and I didn't want to miss out on any opportunities back in Los Angeles.

After playing redneck with my family for a long weekend, it was time to come back to reality with a quick stop in Atlanta before heading back to LA. I sat down with my business partner and good friend at the time, who happened to be from England. We had been developing a show for a while, but this meeting turned into more of a personal one, as he could see my spirits were low. He mentioned that I didn't seem myself, and though I tried to laugh it off, I eventually burst into tears. British people don't do well when others cry. Hell, I don't do well when others cry, or even when I cry myself. Maybe I had been born on the wrong continent. Maybe I was a Brit at heart. I had just had a wonderful vacation with my sisters, work was going well, yet I was bawling. And what about? Between big gulps of air and wails, while looking like a three-year-old who just had a candy bar stolen from them, I explained to him how I didn't understand what I was doing wrong and how I couldn't keep someone interested in me longer than three weeks. What was wrong with me? Was I just not pretty enough? (Here goes the damn pretty line again, for crying out loud. Literally!) Was I too smart? Was I too dumb? Was I not skinny enough? (Thanks for the self-confidence, Mom.) I went into explaining how I understood that I had a bold personality, and that can be intense for some people, but that at the end of the day, I really am a flexible person. I just didn't understand why a unique person like me couldn't find another unique person out there to date. I felt defeated. I had succumbed to the idea of focusing just on work for 2018, since the idea of meeting anyone or even putting myself out there like I did in 2017 no longer felt worth it. My partner mentioned online dating, and I scoffed. *Absolutely not.* "I've done that on and off for years," I explained. I wouldn't consider doing that again. But then he mentioned something I had never thought of. "Lauren, what about international dating? You're always traveling, and you really were born on the wrong continent." *(Did you just hear what I said in my head?)* "You get along with Europeans. Why don't you go on the BBC website and look up the best dating sites?" I really couldn't see where he was going with this. "What is going to be different? There will just be the same guys that I find in Los Angeles," I puffed. "Well, just think about it," he said quietly before we decided where we were heading for our Monday funday after our workday.

I caught a flight back to LA and threw myself into a show for a couple of weeks. Things were insane, and when I finally had a night off, I was too exhausted to do anything else and Postmated. I got situated on the coffee table, plopped down on the floor, and opened a bottle of wine. The dog was comfy on the couch, so best not to disturb her. Most of my nights those days were spent with me sitting on the floor, watching

Netflix, while the dog ran in her dreams on the couch or played "the floor is lava" with her toys on the sofa. Tonight was different. I kept thinking about what Biz Partner had said, and since I had just come off a show that had a big international presence, I thought, *What the hell. Maybe this international thing might be different.* So, I started browsing the BBC's top ten dating sites. I was a little disappointed to see that the first few were just like ours: Match, eharmony, OkCupid. I was about to give up when I saw a site called DateBritishGuys.com. *Are you shitting me? This has got to be a joke.* I had to look it up. When I pulled the site up, it looked as if I were looking back into time. It was like AOL 2.0. (And here we were just talking about AIM earlier in the book! My dad *still* has an AOL email address.) This whole scenario was funny as fuck, so I had to sign up and see if there were even real people on this site. (Cue retro dial-up internet sound.) While creating a profile, I noticed that there were some pretty unique ways of answering the questions. For example, in the category for *Wealth*, some of the options were "I can afford to pay my bills" and "Champagne, darling, champagne." Under *Sexual Preference*, a potential answer was "More than once a day if I'm into you." *Oh God, what happens if you're only half into me? Does that only mean once a day? Or every other day?* I was rolling. And by rolling, I don't mean baked. I don't do drugs, remember? I mean laughing uncontrollably. This site could only have been developed by a Brit. Then came the *My Description* part. This is what I decided on:

> Thirty-one. Female. Likes cheese. Looking for her lobster. Prefers dates in workout clothes or stretchy pants. In shape but considered 'average' in Los Angeles and totally fine with it. Likes sports and cars. German cars to be exact. Doesn't snore. Likes car rides, as long as it's not to someone's death, particularly her own. Enjoys traveling to other countries, especially in off-peak times. Sweats a lot. Beware of hand-holding in summer months. Good hug giver. Comes with dog.

If a guy can't get the humor in that, well then I don't want to be with him anyway. By the way, I'll explain the hand-holding. I have sweaty hands, OK? It's a genetic thing. One of my other sisters has it too. We've deemed it *catfish hands*. I've been terrified to hold hands with boys since I was in middle school. I avoid it like the plague. I figured if I was really going to embrace sarcastically dating, then I might as well throw it out there. If there was anyone really reading this worth speaking to, well, they'd come a knockin'. At the time, the site didn't even have an app, which made it easy to not obsess. I couldn't mindlessly search on my phone while I was bored in an Uber or at a bar alone or in the Trader Joe's line. I would allow myself to check it once a day, but when I was busy with work, one day turned into two. I spoke with a nice lawyer, who was a little young for me, so that wasn't going anywhere. I also spoke with a guy who was going through a divorce, and I felt it was best to let him recover, as we all know people really do need time to work through it all. I was starting to think maybe this site wasn't meant for me, and anyway, my one-month trial was about to be up, so I decided I would opt to cancel. Before doing so, however, I managed to see a thumbnail on the home page of a cute guy in sunglasses from Birmingham and decided to give him a wink. About thirty minutes later, engrossed in another website of some sort, I heard a ping on my computer. It was coming from DateBritishGuys.com. There is an eight-hour time difference between LA and England, so if it was eleven p.m. in LA, it must have been seven a.m. there. Who would be sending a message at that hour?

> Hi. Good morning (for me) and also good evening! How are you doing? Thank you for the wink. It was lovely to get it. I see you like German cars. How about Jaguars or Land Rovers? Any particular sports that you love to

watch? Look forward to hearing from
you soon. Xx The Brit

So he had read my profile at least halfway to see
that I like German cars. That's a plus. Asked a couple
of questions, which shows interest. Should I respond?
I worried that would seem pretty desperate at eleven
p.m. on a weeknight. I would hope, after all the time
we've spent together, dear reader, that we know I
decided to write back.

> Hi, "The Brit," I do like German cars.
> I'm an Audi girl myself. I like all sports.
> I see you like the NFL. I'm an Atlanta
> Falcons fan. What about you? I am
> also a football (soccer) fan. Have you
> been to the States before? You can
> WhatsApp if it's easier. This thing was
> built for the dinosaurs. (My number)
> —Lauren

About fifteen minutes went by, and my phone
dinged. It was The Brit. He thought my dinosaur comment was funny and admitted he was part dinosaur,
but even he knew how to work a computer fairly well.
We were off to a good start. For the next two hours
we covered all the basics: what do you do for work,
where do you live, family questions, as well as the
obvious relationship types of questions. I held off on

mentioning my divorce right away, but it was already in my profile. Clearly, he could read. He was funny. He sent me more pictures of himself, and I, of course, scrolled through my phone to find the best photos of me from the last two months, as one does. As it neared two a.m., I knew I had to get some sleep. These work days were killing me, and I was about to head out of town soon. I thanked him for a lovely chat and hoped we would talk again soon.

I woke up the next day and started my morning as usual, but of course I was thinking about The Brit. It was later there, and he was off of work. What was he doing? Seeing friends? Dinner? The gym? I really wanted to text him, but I knew I needed to be patient. I needed to let him—*bing!* My phone went off. It was him! He was asking how my day was, how I slept, what I had going on for the rest of the day. I didn't want to text back right away, so I waited what I thought was fifteen minutes, but let's be real, it was probably five minutes. We were playing the game. The talking game. The game you do with every app and every situation. Except, we hadn't gone on a date yet. So, this stage is not as dangerous, because if you don't meet, then you only wasted some time texting someone, and no actual feelings played into it. Or the guy acts like a D-bag and ghosts you. Of course, women do that too! (Guilty!) Over the next week, we chatted every day over WhatsApp. We texted each other funny pictures. I sent him a silly picture of my dog sprawled out on the couch. He asked if it was the rug she peed on once, and I replied, "No, it's my couch. It's from Pottery Barn." And he said, "From the days of yore?" I laughed so hard that no sound came out. I was practically gagging on my own spit. If you have never seen *Friends*, please immediately go watch season six, episode eleven, "The One with the Apothecary Table," and you'll understand. It's like we had our own little moment now. I couldn't send a *Friends* meme fast enough. We were beating each other to the punch. This guy was totally OK with my dorky side. He wasn't interested in me because of my job (I'd had some issues before because people wanted an "in" in Hollywood); hell, he may not have even really understood my job. He didn't seem to care that I was divorced. He just seemed to be into *me*.

We decided to have a Skype date and set it for Thursday night (his time). Although it was morning my time and not an in-person meeting, I got ready like I would be going on an actual date (minus the shoes). I showered, put on a little makeup, blew out my hair, picked out a sweater that was not too revealing (knit it is!) but cute. I set the computer up just right to capture my good angles. I was nervous. This was going to be the first time seeing him live and sort of in person. We decided we would each have a beverage on the call— to help calm the nerves, I suppose. I mean, who can't drink at eleven a.m. in Los Angeles on a Thursday? He texted "Ready?" *Fuck no!* "Sure!"

We Skyped for four hours. Things were so natural, as they always seem to be in the beginning, right? But he was soft. He wasn't aggressive in tone. He was funny. He seemed nervous too. I was a little taken aback by his looks. I understand it's winter and winter bush is all around here in LA, but he looked like a Shakespearean villain with his beard and definitely didn't resemble the photos online. He kept stroking the beard. I wanted to just chop it off. But his smile, even through the bearded trees, was very straight. He had good teeth for a Brit!

Our Skype dates became a regular thing. He was there for me when I was in a car accident. He was there when I got an exciting production gig. He was there for good days and bad. Every night before bed he'd send me a "good morning" message on his way to work, and every morning I'd wake up and finish what I needed to do at the start of my day so I could take a break and talk to him for a bit. We had mentioned the idea of meeting one day. I discussed needing a vacation from work. I was being cautious though. How well did I know this guy? We had only been talking for a few weeks, yet he seemed like such a part of my life already. I was doing everything I had never done in these situations before: being patient, holding feelings back, letting him come to me, being pursued. Everything the exact opposite, except one thing.

I had already had a trip to England planned about a week before he and I started talking. I had a couple of weeks off before I had to take another gig. I didn't tell him about it at first, because I wasn't sure if I wanted to meet him. I knew that if I decided not to meet him, that I'd be OK venturing off in the country on my own like I had done so many times before. London comes a close second to Barcelona in my heart. About a week before I was set to leave, I told him I was headed over there to visit friends and do some writing. He said we should definitely meet and go on a date. I agreed but was very hesitant internally after everything that had happened with Billy the Kid. A part of me thought this whole idea was crazy. Going on an international date. *I will totally get stood up.* I hadn't told really anyone about him. Usually I tell everyone about the guys I'm talking to, but this time I didn't want to get anyone involved. If this went sour, then there would be questions I'd have to answer, so it'd be best to just keep this a secret. If anything came of it (doubtful), then I'd say something. I was going to be in London for a couple of days and then head to Warwick to finally see Warwick Castle and then on to Oxford. He mentioned that Warwick was only thirty minutes from his job, so if we wanted to meet up for dinner while I was there, that would be "brill."

The Brit
Part Two

I remember arriving in London. A mad snowstorm had come through, so everyone was snowed in. I had caught a horrible cold on the plane and spent the first two full days in the hotel room, drinking tea and sleeping. I was stressing about our date in a few days because I was so sick. Not like *"cough, cough,* I'm sick" but like "can't get out of bed, fever, chills, I'm dying" sick. Maybe I should cancel? We had this plan of going on a predate that Wednesday in Warwick, and if all went well, we would spend the weekend in the Malverns, a beautiful area in the countryside. It was a great plan, because if for whatever reason we didn't like each other on

Wednesday, then I could come up with a great excuse not to do the weekend thing. I was going to be doing the castle in Warwick anyway, so my plans were happening either way.

I arrived to Warwick by train, checked into the adorable Warwick Arms Hotel, and did my usual routine of showering, doing makeup, blowing out my hair, using the cool feature on the hair dryer to blow out my sweaty hands (even though he was warned via my profile), picking out a cute sweater (since it was fucking freezing in England, even for me), and getting ready for him to text me that he had arrived at the hotel. We were meeting there and then walking to dinner, as most towns in England are walkable. I had let my friend in London know The Brit's full name and place of work details, and he had even given me his license plate just to prove he wasn't a psycho. I have to admit, that did make me feel better. I was really, *really* nervous. *Bing!* He arrived. I went down into the lobby, and he entered through the doors. My first thought: *he's tall.* I mean, anyone's tall to me; I'm only five foot three. But he was *really* tall. He was also really handsome. *No Shakespearean beard! Yay!* We gave each other a hug. It was a little awkward, but not as awkward as the Gator situation. He was in his work clothes, so he changed in the room quickly, and then we walked to a bar for a drink before dinner. The town of Warwick at night was so pretty under the glow of streetlights. He held my hand, which was high school but very sweet. (By the way, there was no sweating, since it was like thirty degrees out. #handwinning) We both couldn't believe we were finally face-to-face after having an internet affair for so long. I could tell he was nervous. I was, too, and the conversation struggled a little. People probably get on sites like that and talk about meeting up but never actually do. Here we were, actually doing it. The date went great. He kissed me at the end of the night but did not sleep over. We had plans to meet in the Malverns on Friday. I was excited.

I spent the entire day at Warwick Castle on Thursday, and it was amazing. I mean, it's no Neuschwanstein, but it's pretty incredible. I was enjoying my day but also looking forward to the weekend with The Brit. I rolled out of bed Friday, took the train over to the Malverns, and checked in to the hotel we were staying at for the weekend. He had everything reserved for us, including a room overlooking the courtyard and bell tower. I knew we were going to have sex, which made me nervous. Well, I didn't know, but I assumed. I mean, hello—a weekend getaway with someone you're interested in? Fuck Town part two. But he also didn't seem like the type of guy that was just trying to get me into bed. He got off work early, and when he arrived at the hotel, we took a . . . nap. *OMG, is he my soulmate?* I didn't know you could nap with someone before having sex with them. This was the most amazing thing ever. We then woke up and had sex, which was surprisingly good.

We planned to head out to a romantic dinner of Indian food—something to cross off my "fuck it" list! We decided to have drinks in the lounge of the hotel first. He seemed more relaxed this evening. As we were sitting there talking casually, he blurts out a rendition of "Where is this going?" I almost had to have him repeat it, I was so startled. *Where is what going?* Normally, I would think a question like this would come when the weekend was coming to a close, but the horses are off! Now, deep down, I did really like him. Think Billy the Kid but on a more authentic level. Someone that I had become friends with over the last month before becoming romantically involved with. Someone that I talked to every day about random things, personal things, you name it. Did I have deep feelings for him? Sure. Was I in love with him? No. Could that be a possibility in the future? Maybe. I also knew that, at thirty-one, I wasn't getting any younger. I wasn't looking for a pen pal or someone who would just come over to the States randomly in a couple of months or a year and we'd hang out. I was too old for this submarining/ghosting bullshit. I wanted a relationship, which is why I signed up for online dating. I also knew that if this was just a romantic weekend away with someone in a foreign land and then we called it a day, that was fine too. I can have casual adult sex, remember? But I wasn't doing an in-between thing. I was too tired. So, he had asked the question, and everything you just read is what I told him. I expected him to possibly pack his bags and leave or freak out, but he actually said, "Oh, I'm glad, because I really want to give this a serious go, too, and I'd really like to date you." It took me a minute to close my mouth, because I don't think I had thought through the logistics very well, but we did talk throughout the evening, and we both agreed it'd be difficult, but we were willing to try. The rest of the weekend was spent gallivanting through the Cotswolds and Malverns, sightseeing and getting to know each other. I even spent my last night at his house. When Monday came and I had to go back home, I was sad. I had this sinking feeling I wouldn't see him again and that this was just a weekend to write home about. (Or to you lovely people.)

I arrived home feeling down. I missed him. My parents didn't even know about him. Most of my friends didn't know about him. This was probably the biggest secret I had ever kept. I couldn't believe I was even keeping it. I was afraid to tell, because to tell would make it real, and if it was real, then there was a chance it wouldn't work. The odds were already against us. However, perhaps the universe was on our side, because my work schedule changed, and I had a chance to head back to England for a month. To see if this really could be something. I knew if I was going to do this, I would have to tell my parents. I figured telling my dad first was probably easier, and then he could share the news with my mom. I just wasn't in the mood to answer all these questions, especially ones I didn't have answers for at the time. I couldn't believe how understanding my dad was. He told me that if I don't go, I would never know if it could work out. My dad was actually supporting a relationship? In all fairness, he did tell me in Spain years ago that I would meet someone someday. I know my dad wanted me happy, but I was going to England to stay with a guy I barely knew for a month. That was pretty crazy. So I went.

The month went by fast. The Brit and I enjoyed the start of good weather over there. Sunshine and get-aways to London. We said "I love you" to each other on a cool evening sitting outside on a rooftop terrace. We even had a couple of fights. Which I'm happy about, because it showed that we were a normal couple. The Brit and I had a lot of time to figure out what we wanted in our relationship. One of the biggest challenges was that we didn't want to have a long-term relationship spent on airplanes. We had known each other for almost four months by this point, and even though that was a short period of time, having been married before, I knew what I wanted in someone. This is what I had been looking for the last four years.

I had to fly home for a wedding. When I was home, I pulled my dad into the office and sat him down. I explained to him that The Brit and I had fallen in love and that things were pretty serious. Dad was very happy for me. Then I told him we wanted to get married. You know the scene in *Father of the Bride* where Steve Martin starts freaking out? I thought my dad was going to start doing that, but he took it quite well, considering. Me going to England for a month was crazy, but this . . . was even crazier. I had gotten control of my impulses. This wasn't an impulse. We had thought this through, talked through many angles of how things could go, when it would be best to do it. There were many discussions over the course of many weeks. My dad was surprised, but once again, he supported me. That man deserves a medal. We went to dinner with my mom that evening to share the news. I was so hoping he could tell her without me. My issue with my mother is mostly that she can be very judgmental at times. I suspect she doesn't realize this. It's hard to be around someone like that sometimes. It doesn't mean that I *can't* be around her, or that I don't love her, I just can only do it in doses. She has a good heart, and as I've gotten older, I've been able to let some things go, but some wounds are harder to heal from childhood, and maybe that's on me. She and I continue to get there, slowly. But on this particular evening, we told her, and sure enough there were a lot of questions. As there should be. After much discussion, I was excited for them to eventually meet him, which would be two days before we got hitched.

The wedding, which took place at Atlantis in the Bahamas, was certainly unconventional. And by wedding, it was more like I had a $200 dress from David's Bridal, my mom was like a swarming bee around us on the beach taking videos, and our wedding dinner took two and a half hours to arrive to our table at the restaurant. It was a disaster. Nothing like I had envisioned. I felt like Charlotte from *Sex and the City* when she marries Harry. Second weddings aren't what they're cracked up to be. But the only moment that really mattered was getting to marry my best friend. The Brit cried the whole ceremony. The rest of the day wasn't what we were hoping for, but those ten minutes that we were standing there, holding hands, and saying our vows were what I've been wanting for my whole life. It wasn't at all like my first wedding. It didn't feel like a show. Of course, it wasn't what I had envisioned, but it felt more real when we said, "I do." There wasn't a huge crowd, but that just meant I could focus on only him. I truly believe I married my lobster.

Epilogue

I have made a lot of mistakes throughout my life, and I bet I'll make a few more. Although I write about my pain in this book, others have their sides, and I'm sure they have pain as well. Perhaps one day they'll decide to write their own books about it. It's OK to fuck up in life, as I've said before. I choose to look back at my past experiences with a twist of humor and growth to implement change. Some of you may relate to some of these situations. Some of you may be going through a divorce or breaking up with a friend as we speak, or maybe you want to move to a big city. I encourage you to not be afraid to figure out your authentic self, because life is way more fun once you do. I had more fun when I let go of trying to be the person my family wanted me to be or what my high school had perceived me to be or conforming to what I thought a guy wanted in a relationship. I wouldn't have looked twice at The Brit if I had met him a year after my divorce. Or during my Kansas phase. You don't want to be stuck in a you you *think* you are and wind up with a Kansas, do you? You want to be the person you *actually* are and wind up with The Brit. I'm telling you (and others will too) that time waits for no one. This doesn't mean you have to join an international dating site and fly off to Europe to go on a date. And also, forgive your parents. My mom and I have come a long way since childhood. That doesn't mean that it's easy all the time, but at the end of the day, they are in your corner. Think about it. That's all. Just know that your mistakes may be memories, but that doesn't mean you have to allow them into your new adventures in life. Make new mistakes. Learn from those. Always keep learning. Always keep growing. Always keep investing in yourself. And always keep looking out for new bed frames.

ABOUT THE AUTHOR

Photo © 2019 Barry J Holmes

Lauren Peacock has worked as a producer in the enter-tainment industry for a decade and has collaborated with such clients as Wiz Khalifa, Snoop Dogg, Lindsey Vonn, and Emmy-winning director Reed Morano. She received a BA in communications–media production from Flagler College in Florida. With a background in theater, she has always gravitated to channels for cre-ating and sharing stories. This is her first book. She currently lives in Los Angeles.

Made in the USA
Monee, IL
27 October 2020

46176546R00090